NAVIGATING
LIFE

book 3

Resources, Direction & Answers for
Understanding Personalities,
Idiosyncrasies & Fears, Marriage Necessities,
Marriage Counseling...Why/Why Not?
What Keeps People from Counseling,
Domestic Abuse and more...

NAVIGATING
LIFE

When and How to Involve a Professional

CRAIG T. MITCHELL, LCSW

NAVIGATING LIFE: Resources:Resources, Direction & Answers for Understanding Personalities, Fears, Marriage, Domestic Abuse and more...
by Craig T. Mitchell, LCSW
©2019 Craig T. Mitchell, LCSW

Edited by Mylynn Felt, Joan Williams and Natalia Burdett
Cover design by Dan Pitts of Dan Pitts Design
danpitts.com
Interior book design by Russell Elkins of Inky's Nest Design

ISBN: 978-1-950741-02-1

Published by Inky's Nest Publishing

1st edition
First printed in 2019 in the United States of America

CONTENTS

Acknowledgments

I would like to thank many individuals who have been instrumental in shaping the direction I have taken in this life. First, I would like to thank my family. My parents provided an example of hard work. They were always there to back me up when I needed support, and they also provided no small amount of help in the form of more hard work on my behalf. My wife, Arlette, was instrumental in teaching me about loving everyone, especially those with special needs. She was truly a Saint who advocated for and took these individuals into our home to give their families needed rest from around the clock care. She was loved by those she cared for and their families. She was also a great mother and disciplined our seven children with tough love when it was needed. My children grew up loving each other and were very patient to accept the other children who came into our home on a regular basis. I am so proud of the contributions they are all making to this world.

One of my high school teachers, James Dorigatti, was instrumental in leading me into my profession as a therapist. The most prominent teachers in my life are Dr. Gary Carson, a psychology professor from college, and JoAnn Larson from graduate school. I can't put in words the inspiration these two people have been to me. I have tried, unsuccessfully, to emulate their professionalism and want them to know how much they influenced my career choices.

I want to thank my patients who over the years have been the reason I love to do therapy. I have always tried to be the best therapist I could for them. I know for some I was not a good fit, just as all doctors or products are not the best for everyone. In these cases, I tried to send them to others who might be better for them. I have learned everything from them and thank them for trusting me to help them get to a better place in life.

I thank my friends who have been there for me, from high school to today. I thank Mylynn Felt, my first editor, Joanie Williams for her input and editing, and Natalia Burdett who was my final editor. I also thank Stephanie Stockdale for her encouragement and prodding during the past several years. I need pushing and she provided it. I am grateful for Russell Elkins and Dan Pitts for their professional guidance and professionalism. I thank Matt Anderson for his work on the illustrations. Most of all I am grateful for the constant prompting from the creator of us all and the blessings of having such a variety of professional and life experiences, which I believe prepared me to write these books.

chapter one

UNDERSTANDING OUR PERSONALITIES HELPS IN MANY WAYS

I was driving with my wife some years ago and it was a two-hour trip, so we had a lot of time to talk and listen to music. Not too long after we left my wife asked if I would mind listening to a talk she had about what was called, "*The Color Code*." It is now called, "*The People Code*." She had brought this up a few times before, and I was not interested because in my profession I had seen of a number of these personality profiles which place human behavior into four groups or quadrants. I thought I had heard all of them and I didn't want to turn this mini vacation into a boring afternoon. She went on to say how much she had enjoyed the author who had come to her school district and spoken to the staff. I reluctantly gave in and said I would listen, and she happily shoved the talk into the stereo. The speaker's name was Dr. Taylor Hartman, and as I listened I found him to be quite entertaining. I was amazed at how he nailed down personalities. As I continued to be more open to his explanations and examples I said, "No wonder I want to strangle that son of mine." (I am kidding, but I was frustrated with my sons at times). I began to get a glimpse of his way of describing people that made sense. His descriptions were organized in such a way that it was easy to pin down people by identifying their specific behaviors. Dr. Hartman goes much deeper and considers our core motives which are the reasons we do what we do.

In a nutshell, here is how his book works. After the initial remarks explaining his methods, Dr. Hartman has you fill out a questionnaire and based upon how you score he identifies which of four different personality types you are. These categories are described with four different colors: Red, Blue, White and Yellow. You can have a primary color and a secondary color. You then go to that chapter and read the absolutely uncanny description of what you are like as a person. This is an amazing process and is very revealing if you aren't afraid of seeing yourself in a sort of mirror. Who of us would not be better individuals as we understand our own selves? Go ahead and get a copy of this book whether you go to the library, pick one up at a bookstore, or on your electronic device. I promise you, you are going to be amazed even if you are Red. You won't understand that unless you get the book and find out what a Red is.

As you read the description of your major color you will see how accurate it is. It is particularly helpful because at the end of the chapter for each color, Dr. Hartman has brief descriptions of the traits each color exhibits in many areas of life. You will learn what your strengths and weaknesses are. You will be able to see what your partner's strengths and weaknesses are as well. The do's and don'ts in a relationship are also indicated. This is very helpful information for all of us. We may also have a secondary color which makes us unique. Knowing this other quality is critical to understanding ourselves and those we love. Later in the book you will also find an area where he also discusses how two people interact based on their colors. This can help tremendously in understanding how to get along and what to expect from each other.

I have used this book to help individual clients better understand others and/or themselves. It can be invaluable in couples counseling to appreciate, and at the same time, accept each other's differences. I also use this book in helping parents to be more effective in dealing with their children. I find it to be an extremely helpful addition to a parenting course. When parents learn about themselves and then are able to correctly identify what color their children are, they become enlightened with new understanding and direction about how to deal with even difficult children. This happens because they receive insight into what the core motives are for each child and, as they learn more, they see more clearly, what to do and what not to do. Combine this understanding with knowing themselves better, and they realize why they may have struggled with their children in the past. Good luck!

chapter two

HOW WE DEVELOP OUR INDIVIDUAL IDIOSYCRACIES AND FEARS

I ran across a book many years ago which explained very clearly, in two paragraphs, why we do the things we do. For example, the authors discussed how we develop our fears, our sensitivities, and the quirks in our behaviors. This has come in very handy as I speak to my clients regarding how they developed the problems that brought them into therapy. The book I am referring to is *Frogs into Princes*, by Richard Bandler and John Grinder. This is just one of their books on the subject of Neuro Linguistic Programming. I have found that when people hear this explanation of human behavior it makes sense, and they are able to recall the genesis or beginning of their struggles.

I explain to my clients that once we read these next two paragraphs they will be able to pinpoint when and where their problem started. Just understanding this very critical point helps them to logically see how they got where they are, and it makes positive change come easier. Before reading I like to cite an example of what I mean. I have had a number of patients who have had this same experience and I find it effective to demonstrate the principle. A child in elementary school does not do well on a test and is singled out and embarrassed in front of the class by the teacher. After this very embarrassing experience the child takes into adulthood a fear of speaking in front of groups of people, a fear of being asked to read in front of others, or a fear of responding to a question in any class or group situation. This fear could also extend to include test anxiety or lack of trust in authority figures. The child grows older and bigger, taking with him or her one or more of these fears into adulthood. If you have a fear and think about it long enough you can generally come up with the first time you felt such a fear.

Frogs into Princes

There are many, many useful ways of organizing the whole process called psychotherapy. One of the ways that is quite simple, and therefore elegant, is to treat every psychological limitation like a phobia. A person who has a phobia made a decision, unconsciously, under stress, sometime earlier in their life in the face of overwhelming stimuli. They succeeded in doing something that humans often have a hard time doing. They succeeded in one-trial learning. Every time that set of stimuli comes up again later in their life, they make exactly the same response. It's a remarkable achievement. You change over the years, and despite the external contextual changes, you are still able to maintain that stimulus-response arc.

The thing that makes phobias sort of interesting is the fact that the responses are so consistent. If a person says 'I can't be assertive around my boss,' they are essentially saying 'somewhere in my personal history I have an experience or a set of experiences on being assertive. I cannot get to that resource in the context of my boss.' When a person responds with the phobic response to a snake, that's a similar situation. I know that at other times in their experience, in their personal history, they have been able to be quite calm and courageous. However, in the context of a snake they can't get to that resource.[1]

1   Bandler, R., Grinder, J. (1979). *Frogs into Princes, Neuro Linguistic Programing*, page 109., Real People Press. ISBN-13: 978-0911226195

I think this makes the point very clearly that our fears have a start and, in most cases, that start takes place in childhood. Granted, there are situations even as adults where difficult and traumatic experiences cause fears to develop. The good news is that we can extinguish these fears with psychotherapy. This is explained in Book 1 in the chapters dealing with depression and anxiety as well as other areas in this book. The following is another method of understanding how we interpret our experiences to limit ourselves.

A Course in Miracles

Sometime ago I was introduced to a book by Helen Schucman and Kenneth Wapnick called, *A Course in Miracles.* This book has remarkable insights for people struggling with true perceptions of themselves and the world. I have used two pages of the preface of this book in therapy since that time, and it has helped many people understand why they think negatively about themselves. I put it here because it is a valuable piece of work that may help the readers of this book to rethink what they believe about themselves. It is valuable for insights into thinking and behavior and subsequently overcoming our anxiety, depression, and fears.

What makes this book so fascinating is that Dr. Schucman was agnostic prior to her experiencing an inner voice that dictated to her the contents of *A Course in Miracles.* In many ways this was disturbing to her because what came to her mind as the contents of the book were not her personal beliefs at the time. Here are her comments:

> *Nothing real can be threatened.*
> *Nothing unreal exists.*
> *Herein lies the peace of God.*

This is how *A Course in Miracles* begins. It makes a fundamental distinction between the real and the unreal, between knowledge and perception. Knowledge is truth, under one law, the law of love or God. Truth is unalterable, eternal and unambiguous. It can be unrecognized, but it cannot be changed. It applies to everything that God created, and only what He created is real. It is beyond learning because it is beyond time and process. It has no opposite; no beginning and no end. It merely is.

The world of perception, on the other hand, is the world of time, of change, of beginnings and endings. It is based on interpretation, not on facts. It is the world of birth and death, founded on the belief in scarcity, loss, separation and death. It is learned rather than given, selective in its perceptual emphases, unstable in its functioning, and inaccurate in its interpretations. From knowledge and perception respectively, two distinct thought systems arise which are opposite in every respect. In the realm of knowledge no thoughts exist apart from God, because God and His Creation share one Will. The world of perception, however, is made by the belief in opposites, in separate wills, in perpetual conflict with each other and with God. What perception sees and hears appears to be real because it permits into awareness only what conforms to the wishes of the perceiver. This leads to a world of illusions, a world which needs constant defense precisely because it is not real.

When you have been caught in the world of perception you are caught in a dream. You cannot escape without help, because everything your senses show merely witnesses to the reality of the dream. God has provided the Answer, the only Way out, the true Helper. It is the function of His Voice, His Holy Spirit, to mediate between the two worlds. He can do this because, while on the one hand He knows the truth, on the other He also recognizes our illusions, but without believing them. It is the Holy Spirit's goal to help us escape from the dream world by teaching us how to reverse our thinking and unlearn our mistakes. Forgiveness is the Holy Spirit's great learning aid in bringing this thought reversal about. However, the Course has its own definition of what forgiveness really is just as it defines the world in its own way.

The world we see merely reflects our own internal frame of reference--the dominant ideas, wishes and emotions in our minds. "Projection makes perception." We look inside first, decide the kind of world we want to see and then project that world outside making it the truth as we see it. We make it true by our interpretations of what it is we are seeing. If we are using perception to justify our mistakes--our anger, our impulses to attack, our lack of love in whatever form it may take--we will see a world of evil, destruction, malice, envy and despair. All this we must learn to forgive, not because we are being "good" and "charitable," but because what we are seeing is not true. We have distorted the world by our twisted defenses, and are therefore seeing what is not there. As we learn to recognize our perceptual errors, we also learn to look past them or "forgive." At the same time we are forgiving ourselves, looking past our distorted self-concepts to the Self That God created in us and as us.

Sin is defined as "lack of love" (Text, p. 11). Since love is all there is, sin in the sight of the Holy Spirit is a mistake to be corrected, rather than an evil to be punished. Our sense of in-adequacy, weakness, and incompletion comes from the strong investment in the "scarcity principle" that governs the whole world of illusions. From that point of view, we seek in others what we feel is wanting in ourselves. We "love" another in order to get something ourselves that, in fact, is what passes for love in the dream world. There can be no greater mistake than that, for love is incapable of asking for anything.[2]

2   Schucman, H. (1996). *A Course in Miracles, Foundation for Inner Peace*, Preface x-xi., Viking. ISBN-13: 978-0960638888

I have found that by reading this with clients, they gain a considerable amount of personal insight. They realize that they have made similar interpretations which are inaccurate as well. I hope after reading this that you gain some personal insights.

chapter three

CONSIDERING MARRIAGE?
SOME THINGS YOU SHOULD KNOW

If you are considering marriage, I hope all goes well with your plans and that there are no big red flags. It is impossible to expect two different people, even if they are seemingly well-matched, to not have ups and downs and disagreements. Hopefully, your marriage will be blessed with communication, compromise, and reconciliation. If, however, you begin to have reservations because there is no real give and take from both sides, then this chapter is for you. I hope you will find the following information helpful.

The Best Predictor of Current Behavior is Past Behavior. The Best Predictor of Future Behavior is Current Behavior. Expect the Expected. Don't Expect the Unexpected.

I tell this to individuals who come to me wondering if they are making the correct decision about pursuing a relationship. This concept is particularly helpful when considering marriage or any long-term relationship. Therefore, if the behaviors you see in the other person and yourself are overall good and uplifting, then as I say above, you can generally expect the same behavior in the future; therefore, it can be expected in the future. WARNING! There are exceptions to this, and that is why you need to read from Book 1 the chapter entitled PERSONALITY DISORDERS, before you continue on to a more serious stage in any relationship. If you are sure that the other person does not have a Personality Disorder or even more serious mental health problems, you can feel more confident in your choice.

Behavior Changes in the Other Person After You Fall in Love

Let me describe a scenario of what happens to many people who fall in love. You meet someone; they seem nice, and you like how you feel when you're with them. They appear very genuine and interested in you. All goes well and you develop very strong feelings and fall in love. Sometime after this you start to notice changes in his or her behavior. You become confused because this current change in behavior seems out of character compared to how he or she acted when you fell in love. You think it is something that will just pass; however, it continues on, intensifying your confusion between loving feelings and fear.

If he or she seems self-absorbed and you find yourself constantly torn, look out! This behavior is much more likely to increase after marriage when a desire to impress you has run its course. If you have frequent sadness, disappointment, and fear prior to marriage, you are highly likely to feel the same after marriage, only to a greater degree. The problem is that many people get hooked into the relationship, fall in love and want to believe the other person's behavior will get better or return to the same behavior they experienced at the beginning of the relationship. They tend to put up with all kinds of inappropriate behavior thinking it will change. Remember the statement above: The best predictor of current behavior is past behavior. The best predictor of future behavior is current behavior. Expect the expected. Don't expect the unexpected.

Once you're married, the unmotivated spouse doesn't have to cover up his or her hidden motives any more to manipulate you into the relationship. He or she now has you in a marriage. What then, is the incentive to dazzle you with any more self-sacrifice? In other words, don't delude yourself into thinking that he or she will change just because you have a ring or are living in the same place. Most people have real difficulty making major changes in their behavior therefore, be careful. Another way to put this is, what you see is what you get, before and after the marriage. Remember what I said about what to expect?

If you are thinking, "I can change him or her and all I need is time," please don't kid yourself. It is highly unlikely that you or anyone can change another person. They must desire to change themselves. If you are reading this now and have not made a permanent commitment, and you have plausible concerns, please step back and think very clearly and objectively. Go get some professional help. Humans are creatures of habit with long-term behavioral processes, and we generally do not make expansive changes in our lives unless we, as individuals, desire to make those changes. Most often, we need to have our world shaken, get religion, or have an ultimatum which might mean the loss of marriage, job, or whatever is important enough to us before we make change. Even then, changes come slowly and in increments, step-by-step. Just because you love someone don't deceive yourself into thinking you can change him or her. When a person is in love they are not in the best position to be objective. I am not telling you to leave a relationship; I am trying to get across the point that we need to be more aware of what is true for the majority of us.

What is very sad is if there is no indication of change in a person before marriage, and after marriage or moving in with someone, he or she changes into a person the other partner does not know. I have seen this enough to believe it is critical for anyone who marries to do a few things prior to marriage. There are no guarantees here, but at least you will have a much more complete picture of each other with some objective information to help you make a more informed decision about marriage. The recommendations I will make are the best way I know of to be as sure as humanly possible about what the other person's personality really is, before you make a life-changing decision like marriage. First, let's examine some real-life examples of situations I have seen.

Examples of People Who Thought They Could Change a Spouse

In the mid-1990's, I had three different females that came to see me about their marriages within a six-month period of time. There is nothing unusual about this except that they all had the same problem. They were all in their mid-to-late 20's and were very intelligent. They each either had or were working on a bachelor's degree. The one issue they all had in common was younger husbands who they felt sorry for prior to marriage. They each believed, while they were dating, that they could change their husbands and make them happy because they, the wives, were strong and competent. To that point in their lives they had been able to control their world quite nicely. During their courtship they discovered these men were all somewhat depressed and had potential but were not consistently being responsible in terms of being employed or anything else. These women pitied them, like seeing cute little puppies with sad looks on their faces, needing someone to take them home and love them. This is basically how each of these sharp young women viewed their younger husbands before marrying them. Reality began to hit these wives right around the six-month mark after marriage. They came to the inescapable conclusion that they were unable to have any impact on their husbands' behaviors. This was a painful and difficult process to come to grips with, this deepening understanding that they were stuck with unmotivated husbands and nothing they could do had any impact to encourage change. We talked about their hopes and options and brought in the spouses to communicate what their wives were feeling. All three of these men were unable to make changes at that time because they either did not see a need to modify their behavior or they did not believe they could change. It does not mean they would not do so in the future. According to their wishes, the goal became to assist these wives to accept the situations they were in and then helping them focus on what they could control. Next in importance was to consider a list of all their options so they realized what paths they could take. Even if those choices were somewhat limited, at least they knew they had some form of control as well as some handle on their own happiness.

If You Have Been Married Before and Are Considering Marriage Again

I tell this to people who have been through divorce and are afraid they will make another mistake by marrying someone who is not what they seem. When you get to the point where you are considering becoming serious with someone, remember you have been through a lot. You have learned much about people and relationships because of your divorce or divorces. The next time you get into a relationship you will be much wiser. You will be able to see things you didn't see before in people. You will sense things you didn't pick up on because you will be more vigilant and, in most cases, that is a good thing. Yes, you might see some things that are not there because of your fears, but you will take things slower and more cautiously. Trust this smarter self; talk with friends or a therapist. It is important to investigate your concerns and fears with a trained professional and involve you future partner in this process. If he or she won't go with you, then I think we both know what that means. (You better think twice).

What Do You Do if You Have Doubts

Getting pre- marriage counseling is always recommended with any serious relationship. There are also pre-marriage seminars that teach couples the basics of communication and other skills they will need in order to deal with the challenges that come with marriage. Many churches have such groups, and they can be very insightful. Do an internet search for pre- marriage counseling and classes in your area. When you find these resources ask about the credentials of the counselor or instructor and if he or she is a licensed professional, as well as how long they have been practicing. Ask about any other concerns you may have and be diligent in getting all the information you can before you decide to start.

The MMPI or Minnesota Multiphasic Personality Inventory

The next thing I tell people who are having doubts about a relationship is probably the most important because it is the most objective way to know about another person's real personality. It will also reveal your complete personality to the other person and yourself. I recommend that early in the relationship you tell the person you are dating that you would not consider a long-term commitment until you both saw a counselor and took the MMPI, meaning the Minnesota Multiphasic Personality Inventory. This is a personality test that has been around since the late 1940's. It has been administered to hundreds of thousands of people, probably millions by now. There is no way that anyone can take this test without it showing exactly what their personality is like. One author who was describing the test said something like this. For the MMPI to not reveal what a personality is like would be like walking through a minefield unscathed. It is amazing in its ability to identify healthy as well as unhealthy personality traits and patterns. It will pick up on mental illness and any attempt to manipulate the test. Some of the major areas it considers are excessive health concerns, depression, over-reacting or being highly emotional, strange thinking, and poor social adjustment, paranoia or suspicious thinking, doubt, fears, indecision, anxiety, low self-esteem, unusual thought processes, peculiar perception, extreme emotionality, social introversion and more. You might be saying, "Anyone can fake a test." Not so with the MMPI. It has been cleverly designed to pick up on any attempt to manipulate it.

Validity Scales Built Right in the MMPI

Within the test are measures called Validity Scales. There are a number of these validity scales which can pick up on attempts at manipulating the test. One is called the Fake Good, Fake Bad scale which identifies someone who is trying to look good or bad for whatever reason. Another scale is the Lie Scale which identifies if someone is outright lying. Another validity scale is called the K scale, one which measures very slight attempts at manipulating, defensiveness, or guardedness or minute efforts at lying or inconsistent responses. If any of these scales have high enough scores they will totally invalidate the results, usually indicating the subject was not being truthful. That is how good this test is. Of course, there are no absolute guarantees because there may be a person on occasion who does not show their true colors, but in my experience, it is amazingly accurate at nailing down a personality. The encouraging outcome could be that you know more of the positive attributes of the other person. It could be that you might discover personality traits you don't want anything to do with. You might even find that the potential partner is dishonest or manipulative. This is the best way I know to be as objective and to know the true personality traits of yourself or someone else. There are always exceptions to anything, but it is unlikely that someone will be able to outmaneuver this test. It is the closest thing I know of to obtain objective information about a person, even you!

Where Do I Find Someone Who Gives This Test?

Psychologists are the most common professionals who give this test. There are some social workers and psychiatrists who also give it, and there are pre-marriage counselors who may have the test also. It is scored and interpreted by a computer program and will have a narrative to explain the results. To find someone in your area who gives this test you may want to search the web for psychologists or counselors. Using the term MMPI in your search may be helpful to find those who give the test. When you call, ask if they administer the test and the fee for taking and interpreting the test. Taking and having the test interpreted will range from $60 to $150 per person depending on where the professional practices. I personally think it is worth that much to answer your questions and have more peace of mind about someone you are planning to spend the rest of your life with. What do you think? Is it worth the money?

25

One last caution here, you need to let the other person know early on in your relationship before you get serious, that you will not proceed into a long-term relationship without going to take the MMPI together. If your partner says no then you should be concerned. If he or she agrees, all the better, because you will both learn much about yourselves and each other. Good luck and be as objective as possible. Make sure you listen to and deal with any concerns brought up by a pre- marriage counselor.

chapter four

KEEPING THE MARRIAGE FRESH TAKES EFFORT

When we start a new relationship, we look forward to dating and hanging out with the other person and spending time together. This one-on-one time is fun and improves the quality of the relationship. Surprise! After marriage dating is still needed to keep two people in love and interested in each other for the duration of the marriage. Until we die! Please do not ignore this critical need because it is vital to keeping a marriage alive and vibrant. It will, very literally, help keep you in love with each other.

Falling in and Out of Love

Few marriages on this planet avoid falling in and out of love over time. This is a phenomenon that has been written about and studied by many people. Don't be surprised if it happens to you because it is normal and you can do something about it. I have suggestions in this chapter and elsewhere in the book regarding how to keep your marriage strong and on course. It is human nature to get off course, on occasion, but don't let that discourage you. If you are resolute and committed, together you will make it work and fall back in love. This is much like going through other cycles in life; hang in there and give your relationship effort by spending one-on-one time together. With children, work, bills, and other stresses, couples drift emotionally and physically away from each other. Don't let it throw you. Decide now to date each other once a week and never stop dating. It is like keeping a fire going; you have to keep throwing more wood on it to keep it burning.

Dating

Many years ago, when I first started doing therapy, I was shocked when I asked couples in therapy a simple question. How often do you date (each other)? By far the most common answer was, "We don't remember." It remains the same after all the years I have practiced. I have been amused when couples tell me, very proudly, that they go out once every month, as if that was going to impress me about the frequency of their dating. Folks, this doesn't cut it; we have got to be more committed to marriage, and part of that commitment is giving romance a chance to keep our relationships together. In most cases, when couples stop dating and working on the relationship, it will go out like a fire. It needs constant feeding with fuel to keep the fire going. Romance and emotional intimacy are the fuels vital to the marriage, and they need careful and frequent application in the right place, before the heat is gone, to preserve the constant warming, nurturing, and excitement we experienced in the beginning. I promise you if dating stops it will become very easy for spouses to become discouraged and disillusioned, causing them to fall out of love either temporarily or permanently with the other.

Friday Is Date Night

Each Friday I became distracted many times during the day as I was working because I was so excited to go out with my wife on our date night. This was something we really loved, and you should get into the same habit, not letting anything get in the way. Yes, at times we had other commitments with our children on Fridays, but if that was the case, we would make sure we were out on Saturday night to not let a week go by without being alone together. We also tried to go for an overnight trip once a quarter. It is amazing what this does for a marriage. Date night does not have to be expensive; it can be just window shopping and dreaming about what you would buy if you had plenty of money. We used to have dinner and do a movie, but you can be creative and one week the wife gets the babysitter and decides what you do. The next week the husband takes his turn.

The "If He Loved Me He Would Know What I Am Thinking" Fallacy

It is time to introduce you to a major mistaken belief that is often incorporated by women. They believe, "If he loved me he would know how I feel, what I want, what I need, etc." Because of this erroneous thinking, usually on the part of women, they try to drop little hints for their man, believing it is a valid test of how much he really loves her. These forays into the deep, dark abyss of the male psyche that I call "Total Cluelessness," can only end in disappointment after disappointment for most women. **Ladies you must understand that for the most part we, as men, are simple, dumb creatures who think we are smart but we don't have a clue when it comes to what you think or want.** Men are concrete, and we only have one program running at a time in our brains. We do not have our "Listen to My Wife" program running when she is dropping crumbs of hints on our poor deaf ears. Please stop this behavior because it will only frustrate you and us. We don't get it. Please don't use this as a test of our love because it cannot measure your man's love for you. My wife used to ask me these kinds of questions like, what kind of candy bar was her favorite or what was her favorite color, and I seldom passed the test. She used to change her mind at times so I became confused when she asked these questions. It really puts a lot of pressure on our poor, simple male brains. Please don't make this the measure of how much we love you, or we will both be disappointed.

Here Is How You Do This Ladies

We need to be told clearly and distinctly what you expect from us, not just once but many times over before we can possibly get it. If you want to tell us something that is important to you, what you need to do is find the right time and place to get the man's attention so that he knows you are serious and need his undivided attention. I know for some women, because of their husband's attitudes, this can be extremely difficult to do. Hopefully, he will be sensitive enough to respond to your sincere request for an audience to tell him what he does not know and cannot possibly understand unless you say it directly. By the way, don't attempt this if he is watching TV or is doing something he really likes doing. The worst thing you can do is ask him in the middle of a game. Some women do this erroneously thinking, as above, if he loves her he immediately will turn off the game and give her his complete, undivided attention. Again, don't make the mistake that this is a test of his love for you. This isn't how men think! We are not tuned into your wavelength! Wait until the TV is off and there are no distractions. Then tell him you need to say something important and ask when would be a good time to get his full attention.

If you can't get him to listen then try telling him what you want in another way. Use the communication format used in other chapters of this book. Express a feeling, be specific about what you want to say and then the reason why or because.

Example

This format for discussion and communication is explained in detail in the chapters on MARRIAGE COUNSELING, WHAT IS IT LIKE? and A BRIEF EXAMPLE OF A PARENTING COURSE and others.

- I feel loved, or excited, or pampered

- When you tell me that you love me or when you fill the dishwasher

- Because it makes me feel safe and secure or because it lets me know that we are partners and share equally the responsibilities around the house.

What this does is focus on and reinforce the positive and at the same time makes it more likely that their behavior will happen again and again.

- This is also effective if you tell him the things **you want him to do.**

- It would really make me feel happy or relieved

- If you would take out the garbage can the night before it is picked up

- Because it is too heavy for me when I am this pregnant, and sometimes you don't have time or forget when you leave for work in the morning.

You can slip these things in all the time, and they are not negative or confrontational. Hopefully, over time, they will encourage changes in his behavior.

Men, What I Call, Hot Tub Therapy Is What Your Wife Needs

Now I will talk to the men out there in an attempt to get them to listen more closely, at the same time trying to cultivate in them some sensitivity and awareness. When she does what I have asked her to do above then, by all means, listen and try to understand what your sweetheart is saying and feeling. Give it some effort, some real, honest-to-goodness effort. It is hard to do, but it can be done, and it pays off in dividends of many kinds, I promise you.

Let me share with you what I learned to do with my wife several years ago. She loved to have a bath in our two-person jetted bathtub. She would get in there and bring the temperature up way higher than I could stand, and she would stay there for hours at times. We decided it was the perfect place to let her share with me what she was thinking and feeling. After she had been in there for a while, she would call me in for what we came to call, Hot Tub Therapy. The rules were that she would talk, and I would listen without giving any feedback or attempts to solve her concerns. I Would Only Listen! Now men, this is not an easy thing to do because for the most part we, as men, are fixers. When we see there is something that is broken (or a problem) we want to fix it. Women are not this way. All they want us to do is listen, and they don't want solutions unless they ask for them. (There are always exceptions to this for both men and women, but generally this is how most of us are).

This is hard for us men to wrap our heads around, but women, most of the time, just want to talk and don't want a fix. This does not make sense to men, and when you first try to do this without trying to fix her, it will take all your powers of self-discipline to not express your opinions. This was hard for me, and it took all the self-restraint I could generate to not offer a way to solve her concerns. Men, just listen, keep eye-contact, let her know you are following her with a nod or a statement to clarify something she said once in a while, but don't try to fix anything or offer opinions. **This is not your time to share; it is hers.** When she is done, I promise you she will be relieved and comforted, and she will feel like you really do love her. I also promise you will be a bit conflicted and frustrated emotionally because you have battled your desire to create solutions for the woman you love. Good luck! Let her decide the time and place where she can open up to you and let her go. If she asks for a solution when she is finished then go ahead and communicate back to her as outlined in, MARRIAGE COUNSELING WHAT IS IT LIKE and apply some problem-solving skills. You can even ask her if she wants some direction before she begins or after she finishes, but let her decide. Then you need to let it go, even though you might be thinking, if she would just do this she wouldn't have to struggle so much. Yes, just breathe and let it go. Get this skill down, and you will have a grateful and happier wife.

chapter five

THE DAMAGE CAUSED THROUGH DIVORCE

Surviving an Affair

This is a particularly difficult subject to deal with because it is experienced differently by so many people. On one end of a spectrum some spouses are finally happy to know the truth about what they have suspected for sometimes years, and others are, of course, devastated. The major obstacles which need to be overcome are numerous for both individuals. The one who has been betrayed has lost all trust, and that is the greatest hurdle he or she has to get through if they intend to stay in the marriage. This trust is completely in the hands of the one who betrayed the marriage vows and, therefore, it is something the first person cannot control. It is totally out of his or her ability to influence. In a seminar titled "How to Survive an Affair" by Barry W. McCarthy, he referred to a study, the source of which I do not know, indicating that the majority of affairs are a result of opportunity. In other words, in the course of work (or whatever circumstance) if the opportunity keeps coming up, that is the fertile ground for an affair to happen. To put it another way, most affairs are not necessarily the result of someone who is openly looking for an affair; they are the result of repeated opportunities.

Logically, this information may be helpful to those who are suffering consequences from such a situation, but it is still quite difficult to come to terms with the pain the affair causes. Usually but not always, I see the injured spouse wanting to know all the details of the affair including how they met, where they went, what they said, what they did, etc. Such people can also have feelings of rage at times and want the other to suffer as they have suffered, or they can simply be so hurt that they say nothing for a time. Many victims of the affair (those who have been betrayed) believe they have been played the fool, and they feel like they are somehow stupid for not knowing what was going on. These victims have been so trusting that when the truth comes out, trust is now a stranger to them. Regardless of how anyone deals with such a shocking blow, if they decide to stay in the marriage they have to be willing to persevere despite the threat and constant reminder that they can be deceived and that it might happen again.

I have been in many marriage counseling sessions where the feeling in the room and the dynamics are completely different. Some victims are full of charity, love, and support, especially if the one who has had the affair is clearly remorseful. It can be very hard to tell if that person is truly sorry. Then there are the sessions where there is such deep sorrow from the victim that it has made me, even as a therapist, feel helpless at times to give hope and comfort in the moment. Sometimes this same theme of pain and hopelessness continues for most of the time the couple is in therapy; this is more the case when there have been multiple affairs or if one affair continued on and on. In these cases, it is vital for the one who had the affair to be completely honest and faithful, forever. It takes a lot of time for healing to take place, and just because the offender says they will never do it again, the victim cannot just let it go right away. They need time and no pressure, so any expectation that they should forgive on some kind of schedule needs to be abandoned.

My Naïve View of Divorce

For many years I have worked with people who have come in for marriage counseling and those who have gone through divorce. I have worked with these individuals and their children to help minimize the effects of divorce. We have considered the process of grief and the various adjustments everyone in these situations has to make. I thought I had a good handle on helping these folks and understanding their plight. Imagine my surprise during a three-month period, when I discovered I had no clue how damaging divorce really is to people.

During this time, I was in my own world of adjustment and certain stages of grief because of the passing of my wife in October of 2010. I had been given the phone number of a woman by a friend, and we began conversing through text and e-mail. I found this medium to be therapeutic for myself because I was able to share many of my thoughts that I probably wouldn't have been able to do in a face-to-face relationship. After about three weeks of communication, she shared that she had been divorced twice and the second marriage lasted only six months. She said she became a statistic. As we began to share more about our lives, I noticed she began to end her e-mails with the same phrase: "I am trying to prevent fear and trepidation from closing my doors." This was a recurring theme until eventually she said she did not want to pursue a relationship. Now, granted, I realize that my charming personality may not have been charming to her. It is also possible that what I said to her in these e-mails may have pushed her away. However, when we reached the stage where it was potentially leading to a deeper level of sharing, I sensed she began to run into a barrier. I believe that barrier was her subconscious protecting her from more potential harm and pain from another relationship. This was confusing to me because in some of her emails she said she was looking forward to hearing from me. I tried to make some sense of the situation so I could understand more completely what happened. I talked to some of my friends who have been through divorce, some more than once. They began to paint a picture for me of the pain and agony people go through during and after divorce. I was dumbfounded to discover that people who go through divorce experience something akin to, and in many cases as serious as, Post Traumatic Stress Disorder. When this happens, it is so painful that it prevents them from trusting or allowing themselves to open up to another relationship that might cause such heartache again. It is particularly difficult if they have married again and then experience another divorce.

A couple who are close friends of mine have been through eight marriages between them, three for her and five for him. It was my discussion with them that enlightened me regarding how difficult divorce is. They had been married three years, and I thought they were very happy and doing well. When I brought up my experience above with the emails they then shared with me that if they had known before how difficult their marriage was going to be they would not have married each other. This was a huge shock to me. They went on to say how their previous marriages were so damaging to them and that the resulting baggage they brought into their marriage prevented them from getting beyond a certain point in their marriage. I have known one of these people since high school, and I have always considered her to be extremely well-adjusted and intelligent. I guess this goes to show that people can be very good actors even when it comes to fooling good friends about their deepest heart aches. In fact, she has penned the steps I use in this chapter regarding the "Steps in the Demise of a Relationship and Mourning from Divorce."

Trust and Betrayal

As I began to comprehend the depth of this anguish people go through, I decided I wanted to do something about it. I started talking to people I knew who had gone through divorce about their experiences. Within a few weeks I interviewed several people who had been divorced, and I took them through a few exercises, which I use for people who need healing. Along with some research, what I discovered was that divorce destroys trust and it is much more insidious when betrayal is involved. Therefore, lack of trust and fear of betrayal become two of the major obstacles in the lives of divorcees if they desire to remarry.

My friend referred to above has written the outline of a book she will write some day, and I am including it here because this book is a resource guide as well as an educational tool. These stages or lists are similar to the stages of grief but are specific to divorce. They are self-explanatory, especially to those who have experienced divorce, and I look forward to the day when she completes her book. She has two different outlines, and I share them here with gratitude to her.

Steps in the Demise of a Relationship

Joan Williams, B.S. Health Science; M.Ed. Education

In any relationship, even the best and most solid ones, there are steps in building it, nurturing it, and giving it life, or steps in allowing it to suffocate or starve to death. Either way, it is a deliberate act by one or both of the parties.

It is interesting to note that there are hundreds of ways that one can nurture and grow a relationship, and that is why each love story is different and unique, but the path to end a relationship seems to follow a predestined set of steps.

The following discussion is about the steps in the demise of a relationship. Sometimes a small effort toward nurturing the relationship will bump the couple back up to a higher level and can even start them on a path to recovery, even if temporary, and so the speed is hard to gauge. The one thing that is inevitable is that at some point on this downward spiral, if there is not intervention, a choice will be made by one or both parties, to end it.

Relationships are in trouble when the following steps begin:

1. Insecurity and frustration about the relationship or interaction between the parties.
- At this point, most healthy individuals will make an effort to resolve the conflicts. Unhealthy individuals use this imbalance to their greatest advantage to undermine, abuse, neglect, or betray the other individual.

- The main measurement as to whether the relationship can be saved at this point is the investment or commitment each party holds for the other person in the relationship. If one party is selfish, indifferent, or uncaring about the other's needs or wants, then most of the time the relationship ultimately ends. Commitment is the key to the success of relationships.

- If both parties are committed to the other person, more than themselves, then the relationship remains. If only one party is committed, or if neither is committed, the steps in the demise of the relationship will continue.

2. Continued or increased unsuccessful attempts to resolve conflicts lead to mild emotional retreat.

- Individuals begin to examine how they are getting hurt and if they have a part in the problem or conflict.

- Some individuals will increase their efforts to work on satisfactory areas in the relationship in an effort to make them so good, that it masks the unsatisfactory areas of the relationship.

- Some individuals will increase tolerance or go into a state of denial of unacceptable behavior in order to enjoy the acceptable portions of the relationship. Usually this adaptation does not last long but in some cases, it lasts a lifetime. It does not mean the couple is a happy couple or that the relationship is nourished, it is just an unhealthy adjustment on one or both of the party's parts to avoid divorce.

- When one makes accommodations in an attempt to secure the relationship, they usually are giving up on having their needs met and settling for what they have or don't have. This usually leads to a second level of emotional retreat.

3. Relationships affect the self-esteem of both men and women. That is why "being in love" is so exhilarating. When the marital relationship is not healthy, both suffer an increased lack of self-esteem and self-worth regardless of the reasons.

4. The inability to resolve the conflicts or to have continual conflicts increase frustration about the relationship and often result in the following actions:

- Denial of true feelings

- Critical thoughts about the other person

- Acting on selfish wants or needs in order to balance the scale and these will vary depending upon the morality of the individual. The result is an increase of emotional retreat from the relationship.

- Guilt from the "acts of betrayal" or "acts of filling selfish wants or needs" whether they are self-destructive behaviors such as alcohol, tobacco, drug use, spending money, or sexual infidelity, can be overwhelming. Not only can these selfish behaviors damage the relationship but can lead to emotional and financial destruction. These selfish indiscretions cause guilt that further erodes the relationship.

5. Unresolved issues cause resentment in both parties. Resentment for unfulfilled needs, lack of understanding, infidelities, lies, guilt, or any number of problems that arise from the lack of commitment to the other partner. These feelings result in:

- Anger, frustration, communication breakdown, fights

- Retreat, despair, distancing from the other person, thoughts of leaving

- Looking for other relationships

- Abuse or use of alcohol, drugs, or sex to alleviate the frustration.

- Lack of intimacy both sexually and emotionally.

6. Signs that relationship is near it's end are:
- End of daily communication

- Purposeful avoidance

- Separate living quarters

- Emotional distancing

7. Separation ~ Divorce
- Complete emotional retreat. Some individuals find other partners at this time if they haven't already. Morality of the individual governs this activity.

- Anger is directed toward the other individual until the pain of the loss of the relationship is resolved.

8. Loss, despair, loneliness, and mourning are the result of the demise of the relationship. Some feel a comforting release from the stress of the relationship but will still go through a mourning period and will feel the loss.
- For some, the loss is devastating and lasts a lifetime, for others, it is just a short period until they can replace the partner with someone new. The difference is the level of commitment the person had to the relationship and to the other person.

- Most replacement relationships live a short life. One should realize that until the mourning process is complete and their role in the demise of the relationship is realized, they usually cannot nourish further relationships. They tend to seek others that are much like the previous partner and the battle begins again.

9. Recovery
There is no set time period that one should take to "recover" from the demise of a relationship. Each person is different and therefore, the timeframe for each person will be different. If the person is still actively mourning each day and deeply despairing over the loss after two or three years, they should

seek professional and medical help. The stress from the loss can evoke physical and mental illness that require professional help to overcome.

10. The most important part of recovering from Divorce is the person you become after recovery. Let's be clear about recovery. A person never fully recovers from a divorce. There are some life experiences that one does not recover from. The term is a misnomer concerning divorce. No one is expected to ever "get over" the death of a spouse. Why would anyone expect to "get over" the loss of a spouse through divorce? That loss is so much greater because death is usually not the fault of either spouse. Divorce is a failure of both spouses. A person can heal and enjoy the joys of a happy marriage and companionship. There is a word of caution concerning a new marital relationship. A divorced person needs plenty of time to reestablish their own identity. They should take the time to find themselves right down to their core self. Only then can they take the time to find someone that they can establish a trusting, loving relationship with. This also takes an extra ordinarily amount of time and effort. Dating and engagements should be extended to help both people establish the trust needed for a relationship. The divorced person must be healthy enough to answer the questions: 1. "What was my part in the destruction of the relationship" 2. "What would I do instead of what I did" 3. What traits do I have that might be an issue in relationships" 4. What characteristics do I need in a partner?" Once a person can do that and can manage their finances, home, and work life on their own for a minimum of two years, then they may be ready for dating.

11. Depend on friends for companionship until you can establish your own foundation and can meet your own needs. Only then, can a person can be ready to embark on a new relationship.

How Serious is the Suffering People Experience When They Divorce?

There are some people who are happy to get out of marriages for many reasons such as abuse of all kinds, adultery, and being treated unfairly, etc. I believe most folks when they are divorced struggle with several of the issues described above. Depending on the type of marriage or relationship they were in from adultery, being betrayed, treated unfairly, verbal, sexual, or physical abuse, these people develop symptoms of depression and anxiety. The symptoms of depression and/or anxiety can be severe and debilitating. They may become depressed for long periods of time, being unable to function in all aspects of life. The symptoms of depression are listed in the chapter on DEPRESSION in Book 1. The same holds true for anxiety and phobias or fears. They may be unable to enter into other relationships because of the lack of trust and fear of being betrayed again. Even thinking of dating or getting close to another person becomes more than they can bear. If they have been in a very abusive relationship they can have full-blown Post Traumatic Stress Disorder.

I believe there are countless individuals walking through life who are so paralyzed by fear of another relationship that they may never be willing to put their heart out on the line again. We don't see them even though they are amongst us putting on impressive masks of coping but underneath the façade, pain, sorrow, and fear are their closest companions.

A Good Book

Shirley P. Glass Ph.D, is the author of a very good book called, *"Not Just Friends, Rebuilding Trust and Recovering Your Sanity After Infidelity"*. This book might be helpful to those swimming in a pool of tides pulling them from no hope to despair to guilt, anger, and confusion. It is a smart work full of so much information that it may take a while to get through it while in the early stages of dealing with infidelity.

I always recommend that you seek professional help and, if you are so inclined, spiritual help. It may be just what you need, if you are not made to feel guilty.

One final thought is that most, if not all, of the above damage caused by infidelity can also be caused by the use of pornography. There is much to be said about this blight on humanity, however I don't have the time or space in this book to include it here. I hope to do so in a later volume along with many other topics. Know this, that if pornography is part of your world then I urge you to get professional help for you, your spouse, your marriage or your children if it has invaded their lives. This is something that causes great damage to marriage. Do not ignore it!

During the past 5 to 10 years there has been a new approach developed in order to deal with pornography addiction, which can lead to acting out sexually, both are very difficult forms of betrayal for a spouse or partner to recover from. Finding the right kind of help is key to recovery from betrayal trauma and addiction. A Certified Sex Addiction Therapist (CSAT) is one who has received additional training, education and supervision to help those who struggle with the addiction and additionally, some specialize in treating betrayal trauma also. The best way to find someone in your area is to do a Google search for a CSAT in your area.

There is a podcast that addresses this issue called "The Betrayed, The Addicted and The Expert." It can be found by searching in podcast applications. This podcast is meant to provide experience and hope from one who was the addicted, the betrayed and from an expert who is a CSAT. You can also find the podcast at AshlynnandCoby.com. You will find honesty and transparency on a wide range of topics there.

chapter six

COSTS OF GOING TO A COUNSELOR

Before we consider the financial costs of going to a counselor, let's consider the costs of not going to a counselor.

Things We Pay For in Life Because the Consequences of Not Correcting Them Cause More Problems

Do you ever have trouble with your vehicles? Or heating/cooling in your home? Maybe your roof leaks. These repairs are sometimes, if not always, expensive and yet we find a way to pay them. And why do we pay them? We do it because we can't be without them. I recently spent over $1,100 on repairs for my car. I paid these expenses because I needed my car. I have an emergency fund set aside to pay for such situations because I know they are going to happen.

What would be the consequences of not repairing my car? Failure to replace the thermostat could have caused more expensive problems, even engine failure. That could have cost me big time! Failure to replace the brakes may have caused an accident or would have meant more expensive repairs. We aren't happy about these expenses, but we find a way to pay for them. We may have to wait a little longer to save the money or put it on a credit card, but we get it done.

My neighborhood experienced a very bad wind storm, and many houses lost a few to over half the shingles on their roofs. Several people were unable to get the necessary repairs finished for over a month after the storm because the roofing contractors were too busy to get to them. Some contractors were not even answering their phones because they were swamped. Why were people so motivated to get these expensive repairs completed? Because they could see the potential problems if it rained or snowed. Water leaking inside the home would cause even more damage to the things they cherish. Fortunately, it remained cold and we had very little snow. These people were nervously waiting and at the same time were getting their financial ducks in a row to pay for the repairs. They found a way because they could clearly see the potential problems down the road, and they were motivated to act as soon as possible.

Wouldn't it Be Nice if We Treated Our Mental, Emotional, and Relationship Concerns with the Same Urgency As We Do with Those above?

What Are the Costs of Not Getting Help?

If a couple is falling out of love and cannot figure out how to repair their relationship the costs are enormous and tragic, not only to them but to any children and extended family as well as friends. If they don't get help before they lose all hope then the following costs are certainly going to be paid.

Important Note: This, of course, excludes situations where abuse or domestic violence is concerned. If such conditions exist then the issues are much different, and it is critical to secure the safety of those who are the victims.

Financial

Let's look at the financial costs of a separation and divorce. During a separation either the husband or the wife has to find a place to live.

Sometimes he or she can stay with family or friends, which is less expensive, but now the person has to pay more for meals because many people, especially men, don't do much cooking. This is expensive as well as a bit unhealthy. Transporting the children and arranging for visits becomes a hassle and costly just in terms of transportation expenses. Then there are the costs of utilities, rent, and getting another household supplied with furniture, beds, blankets, sheets, cooking and eating utensils as well as stocking a kitchen with food and extra clothes for the kids when they come for visitation and even the costs of laundry facilities. Finding a place where much of the above is furnished is going to be more expensive. Financing two households becomes very expensive and overwhelming. What about first and last month's rent and the cleaning deposit? This can easily run into the thousands of dollars just to get started.

If divorce ensues then you are looking at attorney's fees of several thousand dollars plus the child support payments, the alimony and many other costs for child care, usually for both parents. How much do you think it is going to cost now?

Hmmm... Saving money by not going to a marriage counselor takes on new meaning after considering the real financial costs. It appears to be less of a problem and even trivial when looking at the big picture.

Straight Talk to Men

I am addressing the majority of these comments to the men in the world who are, for the most part, the ones who refuse to go to counseling. Yes, there are always exceptions to this general rule, but, in my experience, women are the ones who are the first to desire getting professional help. All too often they are the only ones who will go to counseling. Husbands don't get on board for reasons I address in the chapter on, Why People Don't go to Counseling. Men, you too often let pride get in the way of learning how to get along. Get over it and become an adult! Go get some professional help for you, your wife, and your children. While saying this I am not letting women off the hook who do the same with regard to pride and won't consider getting help as well. I also caution women to avoid blaming men for their problems and take responsibility where it belongs. Both spouses need to take appropriate personal responsibility.

Mental/Emotional Costs of Not Getting Help

I work with people almost daily who are suffering mentally and emotionally concerning a marriage breakup. They struggle in their employment because they can't think straight or make decisions and cannot keep from thinking about it both day and night. Sleep becomes a problem. Concentration is also affected. They don't get pleasure from things they used to enjoy. They have changes in appetite and have no energy. They can feel guilty and may experience thoughts of death and suicide. These symptoms I have identified are those experienced in depression. They notice their children are having some of the same symptoms and begin worrying about them. Essentially, all members of the family struggle emotionally. The same type of behaviors and feelings exist if people have individual struggles aside from marriage problems. Others from family to co-workers and friends observe these symptoms, and it has consequences for many people who care about them.

Prioritizing Which of Our Human Needs Are Most Important

Our basic human needs start with food, shelter, and safety. This is where the majority of our resources are spent. Next is our need for love and a sense of belonging that comes from family or close relationships. Our need for achievement and self-esteem is next. Finally, we need to develop a conscience and moral behavior and then to look back on our accomplishments and have satisfaction that what we did with our lives had value. These are basic human needs. This is according to Abraham Maslow who was a highly respected and famous American psychologist.

Where does peace of mind come in when considering these human needs? It is second only to our most basic needs. I submit to you that when you or your family is struggling with mental-emotional challenges, doing nothing will cause greater consequences in the future. Speaking to men now, I know how you think. You think you have the answers to most of life's problems. If you don't have the answer you will look for a solution on your own because that is how men are. It is very much like asking for directions; men want to do it themselves and avoid asking for help. Men want to fix things, but when it comes to solving mental-emotional problems they may need more information and direction. I ask you, as an adult, to take this seriously and let down your protective defenses. Seek help if you find yourself at a dead end. You are smart, but you don't know everything. Go get some education in therapy; apply it to make yourself better or to improve your marriage and don't wait until it is too late to save yourself, your marriage, and your family. I am also talking to women who would do the same and will not seek help.

Costs of Counseling or Therapy

I have addressed this to some degree in other chapters. Individual therapy or counseling for depression, anxiety, or many other diagnoses is usually covered by health insurance companies under their mental health benefits. Depending on where you live, counseling will probably be in the range of $70 to $120 or more per session. This depends on the type of counselor you see. If you have insurance, you will likely have a co-pay as you would with any medical provider. Most often the co-pay is the same as a medical specialist. Some counseling centers have a sliding fee scale, and may charge much less depending on your income and family size. If you have Medicaid or Medicare it will be free or you may have a small co-pay. Marriage counseling is most likely not covered unless your employer has an Employee Assistance Program (EAP). Usually, most Employee Assistance Programs are free of charge and provide two to eight sessions to employees.

The number of sessions you will need will depend on the severity of the problem. One to 12 sessions is considered short term therapy. Some people with severe diagnoses and long-term problems may require more sessions. I see people whether it be for individual therapy or marriage counseling for an average of three to eight sessions, some less, some more. If you figure $100 per session, then $300 to $800 for a chance to save a marriage and family seems like quite a bargain. Depending on where you live, it may be less. There are many counselors and counseling centers who will accept monthly payments for services. I do myself and because I do therapy in my home office, I charge less because I have no overhead expenses. Three hundred to 800 dollars sounds like a sweet deal when considering how much it costs to separate or divorce. What do you think?

Most therapists with my credentials (Licensed Clinical Social Workers) charge around $100 or less per session depending on where you live. There are a number of marriage counselors who have various kinds of training. Some of these professionals are psychologists, social workers and marriage and family therapists. I address finding a counselor in the chapter on, FINDING A COUNSELOR OR THERAPIST. Refer to that chapter to learn how to find what you need.

A Last Word of Caution

I am not trying to pressure anyone to stay in a marriage with what I have said here. If your situation is very difficult and you have made a decision for your own sake and that of your children that a divorce is best, then do what you need to do. I believe it is always best to seek professional help, if possible, when you are considering making a life-changing decision. Sometimes people just have to get out in order to survive in situations where mental-emotional abuse, child abuse, sexual abuse, and/or domestic violence are occurring.

chapter seven

WHY PEOPLE DON'T GO TO COUNSELING

Reasons People Don't Get Counseling

I believe in our present culture, the way we view the entire profession of counseling is how people in the past viewed the medical profession. For example, just over a few hundred years ago, many people did not trust doctors and for good reason. The medical profession did not have great success in treating patients in the 1700s and 1800s.

Back in the 1700s and 1800s medicine was not what it is today. If a person in those days had a medical problem the treatment might have been worse than the cure. If you had a fever, the doctor would commonly find a vein, cut it open and blood would be drained from a small amount to large quantities depending on your illness. This was called bloodletting, and it was thought, at the time, that this process would rid the body of disease. If a patient had a cold or respiratory problem, a poultice (strong substances in a paste form) may have been placed on the chest that could actually be powerful enough to burn the skin and lungs. Over time people and a number of doctors began to believe less and less in these methods. As the scientific study of medicine and outcomes of treatment were documented these methods were discontinued. To illustrate the point, let's look at what happened to George Washington when he died.

It is thought by many medical experts today that George Washington's doctors were, in part, responsible for his death because of the strong substances they gave him to inhale and gargle. They also applied poultices with strong ingredients including vinegar and dried beetles to his chest, legs, and feet. His lungs were most likely burned or at least compromised. They also performed bloodletting a number of times. It is believed that he had almost two liters of blood drained from his body, contributing to his death. This was thought to be a method of healing in the "Early American Era," in which Washington himself had strong beliefs. The doctors even gave him chemicals rectally to rid his body of bad bile. The combination of these horrific treatments and his illness killed him. It is thought today that he had acute laryngitis, exacerbated by the doctor's efforts. This is only one story of many decades of remedies administered by doctors who practiced without the insight of modern medical research. Over many decades of time people observed what doctors did to treat disease and many were not impressed by what they saw. Indeed, many people suffered because of the treatments in those times. No wonder there had been such lingering mistrust toward doctors and medicine. Much of this mistrust over the years was justified until the late 19th and 20th centuries, when the scientific method of research began to drastically improve medical treatments. As treatments became more successful, faith in doctors and medicine gradually increased. Over the years more proven methods have been made available to produce many medical miracles which are evident today. As a result, the majority of the population today has greater trust in the medical profession because, for the most part, doctors and other medical professionals have proven to be helpful. There are and will always be exceptions to this, of course. Most, if not all of us, have been cured by medications or medical procedures never dreamed of in George Washington's day. This process of changing mistrust to trust in the medical profession took a very long time of significant breakthroughs in treating sickness, suffering, and preventing death.

Though some nervous patients cling to conspiracy theories or avoid medical treatment due to negative past experiences, most of the population will seek a doctor's aid when needed. Medicine is currently viewed by most of us as a noble and helpful profession. However, when it comes to mental health, we are still in many ways in the 1800s when it comes to our opinions of mental health professionals and our trust in them. Modern medicine has changed our minds with very good rates of successful outcomes in treating our health problems. We have not reached the same place regarding trust in counseling in our society today. I believe close to half of the people in the world today would not enter the door of a counselor for any reason. To their credit, many more women than men will seek help. The majority of my clients, probably 85 %, are female. Large populations of the men in this world believe counseling is for weaklings and those who don't have a brain. My hope is to change this general attitude and to turn the 21st century into the age when logic, reason, and common sense take over, and people begin to do what is necessary to change and make their lives and those of their families better.

How We View Medical Professionals Today

Most people don't hesitate to go to the doctor to get stitches or a cast for a broken bone. This also extends to very serious medical problems. They hardly think twice as they go in for diagnosis and treatment. They realize they will have financial obligations, but they know there may be serious consequences if they don't get treatment. Their condition could become much worse, possibly requiring hospitalization. Extended families may, at times, step in and help pay for treatment if there is no health insurance. Some understand they can apply to Medicaid for assistance or know that emergency rooms will write off part or all of their bill at certain hospitals, or they know payments can be set up to allow time to pay off their charges.

There are exceptions. Some people are stubborn and won't go get medical help because they think they will be fine. Some may not trust doctors or medical clinics. They may not want to go because they don't want to create another bill. When loved ones or friends refuse help we try to get them to see reason and to go to see a doctor, especially if we know the condition they are struggling with may be serious.

Where Are We Today regarding Trust in Counselors for Treatment of Emotional/Mental and Relationship Problems?

As explained above, physicians in the 1700's caused more harm than good in many situations; this led most people to not trust them. It took 200 years for their track record to improve, and we began trusting in them. We are about half way there with regards to trust in the mental health profession. We are about 100 years behind the medical profession in our willingness to seek mental health services. My hope is that we can move along the path to changing this pattern much more quickly.

How Can This Trust Be Changed?

I believe a new direction needs to be taken by the whole field of Mental Health to turn the corner in encouraging people to seek help earlier on when they have mental or emotional challenges. More advertising and statistical data needs to be present in all forms of media to demonstrate how counseling and/or therapy helps individuals and families. Obviously, we need to have more cooperation from insurance companies because they actually discourage people from getting help when it comes to mental health benefits. They make it very difficult by making the process complicated, even denying preauthorized claims at times. I know. I have to deal with them all the time, and it is very, very difficult – to the point that they, the insurance companies, make billing and reimbursement so miserable that many therapists don't want to deal with them. Some therapists go to "pay for service" only because they have such a hard time with insurance companies. I appeal to law makers, as all the new laws dealing with medical benefits are being debated, that they can consider fully the needs of so many who suffer in silence because they have little, if any, voice in what is being decided. While reading this book, I hope you begin to understand the many emotional wounds people can experience. The toll on families and individuals is immeasurable, and we need to make therapy more available to those who need it. There are children and parents who would be so much more productive and involved in life if they had a way to easily access counseling, without fear of being labeled abnormal or crazy. Wouldn't that be nice, to have such an environment to live in? My vision of such an environment would be for people to call a therapist with the same ease they call to make an appointment to see the family doctor. In that world I can hear someone say, "I am calling my counselor to check on some concerns and thoughts I have been having recently." I believe this kind of attitude and access to therapy would prevent many of the tragedies we see in society today because people with disturbed thoughts would have fewer barriers to getting help from mental health services.

In many areas of the country, there are efforts to introduce financial programs to help students in high school better understand how to make financial decisions. I propose that we start doing the same with mental health awareness in schools as early as elementary school to reduce the stigma that counseling creates in the minds of people. Starting early to rid ourselves of bias from racism to all kinds of misconceptions is best done at a young age. If you are a parent or in a position of influence, I encourage you to keep in mind this plea to advocate for mental health awareness and training every chance you get. Your child may be the recipient of such knowledge and acceptance in the future. Let's make the environment friendly for our children and grandchildren to feel as comfortable seeking treatment for their mental health as we are about our physical health.

Other Reasons People Don't Seek Counseling

No Trust in Counseling

Have you ever heard people say that counseling is for the weak and those who aren't smart enough to solve their own problems? These are the people who have no trust in the profession of counseling. I believe they are the ones who are stuck in the late 1800s as far as their understanding of the positive outcomes in therapy. The individuals who have benefitted from a caring and objective therapist cannot be numbered. After being accepted without judgment and then learning the steps to change their distorted perceptions, they have been able to go on with life, comprehending more fully their true worth and value.

I heard a radio commentator a few years ago who said he went to a couple of counselors, and he went on and on about how they were no help at all and that he would never do such a thing again. Obviously, he did not have a good experience and had no trust in counselors. There are many reasons why this may have happened. Maybe he did see two counselors who were not helpful or not competent or possibly he was not ready to make changes. Who knows how many more who were listening that day now have the same opinion. Just because one person did not have a good experience does not make counseling bad for everyone else. I thought about the many people who I have seen over the years whose lives have been changed, not because I am any great sage, but because I was able to show them some proven methods and steps that help to change the perceptions and thinking patterns which got them into trouble. These methods have been used for many years and have proven to be helpful in changing lives.

Financial

There is a financial wall or gap that exists in the minds of most people regarding going to get help for these very critical needs. Let's look at this phenomenon and try to understand what needs are the most important. We pay rent/mortgage payments and utilities and, even though it is difficult at times, we realize we need a roof over our heads to stay safe and comfortable. We pay for transportation such as cars, bus passes, or commuting passes of all kinds. We pay for repairs, gas, oil changes, and other upkeep on vehicles. We will even buy boats, personal water craft, ATVs, snowmobiles, campers, trailers, etc. We pay for the insurance to cover them and the license fees to operate them. We work out at the gym or buy all kinds of personal things that we believe we cannot live without. We buy our kids gifts for birthdays, Christmas, and go on vacations which create wonderful memories. However, when it comes to our mental health or broken relationships we can't afford to even look into taking the first step. Even though we are struggling day-in and day-out and become depressed and anxious, we just can't afford to do anything about it. We will go and buy a new TV because that will make us happy. Then we have to get the latest technology to go with it. I truly believe spending money on any kind of counseling for peace of mind becomes a threat to having all these wants which we have come to think of as necessities.

Do you see what we are doing to ourselves as we ignore these problems? What is more important in life than peace of mind? Maybe a few things, but being happy is not far behind almost any need we may have.

Stubborn

We have probably all had a family member or a friend who has been stubborn like this. They won't go to a doctor because they are not sick enough to require it. They believe they can fight off whatever it is they have. This stubbornness spills over into the areas of, "I don't need any help," especially when it comes to counseling because they don't want to pay a "shrink."

Stigma

We also have the belief that if we go to counseling we will be thought of as crazy. Ever heard or thought these statements? "If anyone goes to a shrink they are not right in the head, and I am not one of those people." "If I go to a shrink then that means something is really wrong with me." "I wouldn't want anyone to know if I did go see a counselor; that would be the worst." Some even fear that a diagnosis received from counseling will be forever attached to their name.

I'm Going to Be Blamed; A Big Issue for Men

What I am about to say is true for a lot of men in terms of how they perceive they will be treated in counseling. Even though marriage counselors normally do not take the approach of blaming either husbands or wives in marriage counseling, men do not want to take the chance of being told they have responsibility for changing the problems they bring to their marriage. I have found that men have a preconceived belief that they will be singled out and that the counselor will be on the wife's side. Some husbands only go to marriage counseling because they want to make sure the counselor knows that he is the sane one.

I know that there are exceptions to what I am about to say, and I salute these men who do take personal responsibility. However, many men have fragile egos and can't bear the thought of being blamed for a marriage that is not going well. After all, they know how to fix things and they don't need help. They believe it is their wife who needs the help. Ask any man, and the vast majority will tell you this. In our western culture men believe they have the answers to everything and to think anything else means they are broken or weak. They can't admit to this because it goes to the core of who they are, causing them to question their manhood. Even though these men don't really communicate or listen to their wives except to give them their opinions, they generally don't change their behavior. Why would you if you don't think you have a problem? This is almost like having a personality disorder which I discuss in the chapter on PERSONALITY

DISORDERS. Women do you understand a bit better how husbands are afraid of marriage counseling? They don't want to be told they need to make changes. This is hard on their psyche, to hear or, heaven forbid, admit they might not be right, or that they might be lacking in some way. Can you see how mortifying and judged they would feel to go to another person and be told in the company of their wife that they need to change? Can you imagine the humiliation they would have to go through to be told this with their wife sitting there, with a smile on her face, saying I told you so? This may sound a bit dramatic but it is true. A man will conjure up the worst scenario he can think of about getting marriage counseling, and I have just described one of them. It is also hard for a man to think that he may be told he needs to be in therapy to deal with his own problems. Even if he knows he needs to get help he will be much less likely to get that help compared to women because of what I have just discussed.

What a Mentally and Emotionally Healthy Man Says and Thinks about Counseling

Listen up Men! I want to address this idea with reference to the military and sports. A man who is confident and strong mentally and emotionally would go into battle to be with his comrades regardless of the odds. We see depicted in movies how those in the armed forces cover and back up each other. They don't leave anyone behind. They are dedicated to their last breath in honoring their vows to protect their country. Movies demonstrate this with scenes of armed forces personnel sacrificing their lives to save their comrades. We have all heard of such devotion in the military ranks.

The same is true in the world of sports. We see examples of individuals working, practicing, and sacrificing for the good of the team. These athletes will spend hours working out in the weight room. They study film of their games and the opponent's games. They work out in the offseason and practice with their teammates when practice is not required. They create goals for themselves and their team to win the conference championship, and they work to achieve these goals a step at a time. They will give every last ounce of effort they can to win the relay race, drive down the field to score with only seconds left in the game to win. This is true for all team sports, this same dedication to team and school.

If a man, or woman for that matter, who has taken a vow to protect his nation can give his or her last full measure of devotion to that country, then why can't his or her marriage and family have the same kind of dedication? Didn't we all take vows to love, honor, and protect, in sickness and in health, until death do us part? Some even make their own vows or take other vows based on their beliefs. If someone is able to give his or her life for a comrade should we not have the same devotion to our spouse and children? Would we not run into a burning building to save our family? I challenge you, as a man, to stand up and be strong and do what needs to be done to save your marriage and keep your children. Do this before it is too late. There are coaches, mentors, and trainers who teach athletes how to move, think, understand, and play their sport. When you got married you didn't get a manual on how to be a husband or parent your children. Go find a coach who can teach you the skills you need, especially when you struggle with the most important teammates you will ever have in life: Your WIFE and CHILDREN. A therapist or counselor is nothing more than a coach to teach you how to understand, think, and play in this most important championship of your life, your marriage and family. These are not easy tournaments to win, but if you are smart and strong-willed, you will think of these relationships in these terms, just as you would in sports or your profession. Get some training and coaching for your marriage from a professional, so you can learn the skills to succeed. Marriage is a lot more complicated than a sport. Doesn't it make sense that some training is necessary? Hopefully, afterwards you can say with pride, I did not quit; I got training early in the game, and I learned exactly how to come up with a game plan. I know what to do when I am confused and struggling and how to adjust at half time. I won't stop, and I won't leave any of my team behind. I will sacrifice myself, if necessary, to do all in my power to not lose one of my comrades in arms, my wife and my children. I will become the leader of my own Special Forces team, and I will lead them with dedication, loyalty, and above all, with love so that none of us are lost. Be the Man, the leader who is unafraid to go into any theater of operations be it a marriage counselor, a parenting class, or whatever training it might require. Be the one your wife and family can look up to and say, "You lead the way; we trust you to get us through this battle without losing anyone." As you do this they will look to you with the same love and respect we all see in our heroes and role models.

Be that man; let nothing stand in your way. You don't have to jump on a hand grenade for your marriage or family, but you do have to act or you may lose them just the same.

Where Does Our Mental Health Stand in Terms of Importance in Our Lives?

When it comes to what we think is important in life, we perceive jobs, money, houses, cars, clothes, keeping up with the Joneses, and modern trends as well as recreation and physical health, to be way ahead of mental health.

Which of the above Items Are Most Important If We Look at Them Objectively?

Having food, shelter, and clothes are very important as well as physical health. Most of us today have the means or know how to access the resources to obtain these basic needs. There will always be those who are in need of the basics, and we need to continue to help provide them with these needs. However, I believe we need to begin to consider how very vital mental health is to everyone and then go forward acknowledging this and feeling good about doing so. Wouldn't it be nice if we had the same desire and drive to take care of our mental health as we do about going to the gym or pursuing a hobby? Think of all the money we spend on workout programs, workout clothes, club memberships, vitamins, supplements, and eating proper foods.

All this with little or no thought about our mental health!

Think about when we or a family member has depression, anxiety, or grief because of a loss in life. During these times our mental health impacts all other areas of our life, sometimes in very difficult and dramatic ways. We struggle to function in our jobs, think clearly, and make decisions. It affects every aspect of daily life. This is when we need support and answers to getting through tough times, not to mention when we or someone we love has chronic or long-term mental illness requiring medication and therapy.

As I was writing about this very issue I received a call from a friend I work with. She has two children, one who is an adult and another who is a teenager. They are both struggling mightily with anxiety and perfectionism, and she knows if they don't learn how to deal with these issues, they will continue to struggle in their own families later in life. They are hesitant to get help, so she has to be very careful as she approaches them in order to encourage them to see me. What parent today does not have at least one child who is having some kind of challenge that we know would require just some kind of objective help to get them thinking better thoughts and improving coping skills? As parents, we would like to give them direction but advice from a parent, with few exceptions, hits a brick wall before it gets near their ears. How do we help them if we don't take care of our own mental health ourselves? I hope we can change our outlook toward mental health and pass it on to our children.

Questions for You

I ask you to contemplate this for yourself. Do you take care of your own mental health or do you simply ignore it? What do you do to improve your mental health? Do you spend any time on it? Do you know what to do? Do you know what it is? Would you go see at therapist if you were unable to work through a personal challenge? What are you teaching your children about mental health through your attitude? Do you and they just suck it up and ignore it? When they are suffering and need help beyond what you can give them, what will you say?

A Simple Test to Determine Your Mental Health

I teach a lot of people self-awareness through the process of relaxation. Many of us don't realize exactly what it is we are feeling in our bodies even though those feelings motivate us to take unintended actions. I had a recent client who was abused as a child, and this set her up for continued abuse by other males in her life, including husbands. From all outward appearances she seems to be quite calm and in control. When I questioned her in depth about this she said she always feels tight, tense, and in a state of hyper vigilance, which is to say that she is always feeling fear. In public she keeps her distance from men and says she jumps out of her skin when someone walks up behind her in a store. I was unable to get her to go through relaxation exercises because of her fears. We did find a way for her to visualize a safe place in her mind where she learned to practice relaxation. Her next assignment was to try memorizing the feeling and reproduce it each day of her life, in all kinds of settings.

Let's see if we can determine, to a certain degree, what your mental health state is. When you have a few minutes to yourself, with no distractions, try this very simple process. Sit back, close your eyes, and try to relax and identify any feelings you have. Now, for each feeling you identify, determine how strong they are on a scale from 0 to 10. Zero would represent a state of complete calmness, almost asleep and 10 being as intense as that emotion can be. What did you notice? Some people don't recognize their feelings at first and have to really tune in to what their body is feeling. Some of us live with these unrecognizable feelings for so many years we don't notice they are there. The interesting thing is that these feelings may be motivating and pushing much of what you do each day. This self-awareness is critical because we may be doing things for reasons we won't understand because we don't listen to our minds and bodies. Our subconscious mind motivates us, protects us, and we oftentimes have no idea it is driving the car, so to speak.

I challenge you to do this many times throughout a week and try to see what your mind and body are telling you. They are both connected, and your mind has a lot of control over what your body feels and does.

Why Isn't Our Mental Emotional Health a Priority?

If you performed the above exercise to identify your feelings and how intense they are, I hope you gained some insight and understanding about your mind and body. So much of our present state of mind is the result of previous experiences, many of which are unpleasant and we would rather not deal with them. Some of these experiences are painful and include abuse, divorce, death, losses of all kinds, being treated unfairly by family, peers, coworkers, etc. I would include here any reason for disappointment or sorrows, which commonly occur in life. Who wants to deal with these things? None of us! We want to shut them out and never deal with them again because they are painful! The problem is, these painful feelings do not, for the most part, just go away, and unless we do something about them to process them and let them go in a healthy way, they are still there like volcanoes building pressure in our subconscious. These subconscious pressures can cause us to do things we don't understand. These pressures can start at a very early age and are forces that cause us to do things throughout our lives without us knowing why.

There is a very simple answer to the above question. Mental and emotional health are not priorities because we don't want to revisit and re-experience pain. This is the paradox. If we don't take care of certain difficult experiences appropriately we may very well struggle with life, being unaware why we feel the way we feel and do the things we do.

Examples

Have you ever had an experience in which you wanted to tell someone honestly how you feel about them? It might be a spouse, child, parent, boss, coworker, friend, or someone who has offended you. Possibly, you are afraid of them or afraid how they will take what you want to say. You may have practiced what you want to say, and you are sure this time you will be strong enough to get it out. Thus, you get yourself built up and have everything in place you need to say and do, but when you get near them you melt into a mound of Jell-O. So much for your well-planned strategy. This can happen despite your desire to change your responses, from how you anticipate taking a test, to how you deal with your child's teacher, to talking to yourself about taking a much-needed break. You tell others to cut themselves some slack but have a hard time pulling it off yourself because most of us don't practice what we preach.

What happens in these situations is our conscious mind knows logically that we need to do something because it keeps coming up in our thoughts until we have to deal with it. Then, when we make a plan to do something about it, our subconscious mind takes over and says no we are not going to do that, and we careen off onto another subject and avoid the matter altogether. When we walk away from the situation we say, "Why didn't I do what I planned?" The reason is because our subconscious mind is there to protect us from possible pain, and it won't let us confront the situation even though we consciously planned to do just the opposite.

Some simple examples of this are when someone is afraid of dogs, and they react with fear and possibly panic when a dog crosses their path. The person secs the dog with its owner coming almost a block away. He thinks over and over, "I am not going to jump out of the way or panic." Just before they pass, however, he backs against a fence and waits for the dog to walk by and starts to exhibit fear, especially when the dog wants to sniff at him.

Another example is when a woman who has been abused walks by any man and gets ready to defend herself each time this happens. She thinks constantly, trying to change her pattern of behavior, but to no avail. If you don't think this happens, you are in dreamland. I currently have a client who does this all day long. She comes across as very professional and together at work, but underneath she is scanning everywhere for any possible threat from any man.

A child who has been physically abused will cower or dodge an adult who is a little loud or assertive because his or her subconscious is always looking for something threatening in the environment. Anyone that looks in anyway like an abuser from the past will cause a defensive reaction.

Working at Resolving Our Problems Is Hard Work

I give the following handout to clients when I detect they don't really want to put any effort into their treatment. It is from a famous doctor/psychologist named Frederick S. Perls M.D., Ph.D.

Psychotherapy and Unfinished Business

"A major problem for all forms of psychotherapy is to motivate the patient to do what needs to be done. He must return to, "unfinished business" which he left unfinished in the past because it was so painful that he had to flee. Now, if he is encouraged to go back and finish it, it is still painful: it reactivates his misery, and from the short-run view, it is still to be avoided. How can he keep at the task-ultimately, how can he keep himself at the task-when there is such a quantity of unpleasantness to live through?

To this question no positive answer exists today for most persons. An unknown number, perhaps a majority, believe they would have no troubles if the world would just treat them right. A smaller contingent does have, at least at times, a vague recognition that they, themselves, are responsible for the ills that beset them, at any rate in part, but they lack techniques for coping with them other than the old threadbare resolution, "to do better," or moral maxims. Or they displace problems from their true arena to a spurious one which allows a great show of busyness and suffices, at least, to let off steam. A very small number take their troubles to an, "expert," hopeful that some magic formula will be uttered and their personal devils exercised.

Of those who start treatment most do not continue. Their cases are not discharged by the therapist but are self-terminated. Many, when magic is not forthcoming from one therapist, try another, then another, and another. Among the myriad ways of expressing dissatisfaction with one's doctor a very common one is to the effect: "He doesn't understand my case." Perhaps he does not, and there may be benefit in shifting. But most patients, perhaps all, wish in some degree to prescribe to the therapist how he shall cure them--and this prescription does not include that they shall suffer in the process!

For surgical and pharmacological forms of medical treatment the patient can be perfectly passive, and it is better if he is. He may receive an anesthetic and wake up with the operation over. The notion that treatment should be administered to a passive patient generalizes to notions of how it ought to be possible to cure a neurosis. The latter, however, is not, "organic," but, "functional." While the patient is not so naïve as to suppose there can literally be surgical removal of his symptoms, he is likely to feel that little more should be necessary on his own part than to bring the body. Once he presents himself, the doctor perhaps with the aid of hypnosis--ought to be able to fix him up.

Since it is, nevertheless, the patient himself who must change his own behavior and thus affect his own cure, all methods of psychotherapy give rise to what, in professional jargon, are called, "disappointment reactions." These usually stem from realizing, after a time, that the therapist actually expects one to do hard work and undergo pain. As a matter of fact, without being fully aware of it, one may have sought out the therapist in the hope of acquiring exactly the opposite, namely a better way of escaping work and avoiding pain. To discover that therapy involves concentrated doses of what once thought to be relieved of seems as absurd as to take the ailment and apply it as treatment.

Likewise, with respect to the pain involved, he comes to see that this is not pointless, needless pain. He begins to appreciate the roughhewn wisdom of the advice to get back on a horse, when thrown, and successfully ride him off. The patient's situation is different in that he has, perhaps, avoided this particular horse for a long time: years, perhaps, or even most of a lifetime. Nevertheless, if healthy functioning requires that he learn to ride and manage a certain kind of horse that has thrown him in the past, the only way he can possibly do this is to make approaches to the horse and then sooner, or later, get into the saddle."[3]

The lesson here is to understand that if you want to get past a problem you must put forth effort and work at it. I almost, without exception, give homework assignments at the end of each session because I know that the normal one-hour-a-week in therapy session is not going to get the person to a better place very fast. If they are working on meaningful assignments during the week their progress is greatly accelerated. Another way of looking at therapy is to think of a person who is recovering from a surgery that requires physical therapy to enable him or her to gain the strength to walk again. If you have ever gone through physical therapy you know it is not pleasant and oftentimes is painful. However, if we want to walk again we put in the time and hard work to gain the necessary strength to accomplish our goal of walking. We see athletes do this all the time after an injury. They work at their rehabilitation to get back to what they love to do. The same holds true for almost any kind of psychotherapy. Hard work and staying focused and committed are necessary to gain the

3   Hatcher, C. and Himelstein, P. (1976). *The Handbook of Gestalt Therapy*, pp. 84-85. Janson Arnson.

strength to overcome our particular kind of mental-emotional injury or challenge. In this book I address the various kinds of work people need accomplish in order to overcome several types of problems in the chapters describing how therapy is done.

A Healthier Way of Thinking about Counseling/Psychotherapy

Think of counseling as a tune up or an oil change. Essentially, what counseling will do is to help you ground yourself in reality and be more logical and objective in your thinking. I recall, several years ago, reading about a study done somewhere in the U.S. in which it was reported that 96% of the population will have, at least one time in their life, enough symptoms of depression or stress to require counseling. Understanding this simple fact, that to need some kind of intervention emotionally and mentally is a very common part of the human condition, may change your view of counseling. I was impressed just recently to read on my daughter-in-law's blog that she and my son decided to go in for some relationship counseling. She said, "We are going simply because we need a little boost in our skills." Can you imagine what this world would be like if we all had this same attitude?

Counseling Is Not a Lot Different Than Going to a Friend Who Cares and Wants to Help

If you think of counseling in another way it may help us to accept and be more open to it. Counseling came to be a profession out of a need to address the problems that are common to the human condition. Simply put, a number of concerned people began thinking about how to solve personal problems in order to bring some joy and balance into the lives of those for whom happiness was lost and not reclaimed on their own. How often do we talk to friends and family to get help for something we are having trouble with in life? It is normal and natural for us to seek advice from friends and family. However, when problems become complicated and require methods and ways to overcome problematic thinking, these good people we turn to may not know what to say or do. They can even give us direction that is counterproductive to our situation. We have all heard those bits of advice: "Just get over it," or "Just do this or that and everything will be all right." You know these people care about you and want to help, but oftentimes their counsel is colored by their own biases. Sometimes they are so close to the situation they cannot be objective themselves. We know that some of these people are not the best listeners, and even though we love them and care about them, they just don't understand.

This is where counseling can pick up the slack and provide us with an individual who is objective and listens without judgment. Counseling can be just as simple as this - to have someone who will understand and accept you unconditionally. Sometimes this is all we need, and once we feel this acceptance we can be on our own way, solving our own problems. In other situations, if we have been exposed to abuse, neglect, depression, anxiety, feelings of inadequacy, a lack of love, or whatever, counseling teaches methods and proven techniques that help people change their thinking to the point where they can begin solving their own problems. At this point they can take control of their lives.

Over the past 50 years a lot of scientific studies have been done to determine how to positively affect mental-emotional health. Let's take advantage of these methods. It has been worked on and refined, and there are a lot of good people out there who want to help others and know how to do so. As I say constantly throughout this book, there will always be exceptions to what I say. There are some therapists out there who are not as competent as they should be. Frankly, I look back at some of the things I said and did in my early career and I shake my head. Because of new research, medications, and methods of treatment I have changed some of my approaches in therapy. I sincerely always wanted to help. I am asking you as the general public to give those who want to help a chance to assist you and your family. Let's change the way we think about counseling/therapy and give it a chance to make a difference in our lives. Go ahead; it doesn't bite.

A Critical Note About Therapy and Therapists

As I alluded to, there are therapists who are better and some who are not as competent, just like any other profession. The thing we need to stay focused on is the fact that there are proven methods that work on various types of mental illness. Some therapists are not as good as others in teaching or directing clients how to use them. Therefore, if you have a bad experience with one therapist don't throw out the baby with the bath water; you need to find someone else who knows how to deal with your particular problem. This is where searching, calling, and asking questions of therapists is vitally important. What I mean by this is to call and ask to speak with the counselor before you make an appointment. If that is not possible then ask the secretary if the counselor has experience in treating your specific area of concern. Some counselors have experience and expertise with certain areas of mental health or diagnoses. By asking these questions hopefully you will find someone who appears to be competent with your particular need. Be bold; ask if they have dealt with your type of problem and don't pull any punches. Don't stop until you find someone who you feel comfortable with based on the answers you get. You should also ask about insurance coverage and fees prior to making an appointment.

If you have a problem with your car, furnace, washing machine, or any other appliance that needs fixing, you have to do some investigation into who does the best repairs affordably. The same goes with your medical providers. If you won't go back to a doctor because he did not listen or if you think he or she did not help, do you forget the fact you have a serious medical problem or do you find someone else to examine you? Of course, you find someone else. Do the same due diligence with your mental health. Trust in the fact that techniques exist to help with most problems; you just need someone who knows what to do with your particular kind of problem. Sometimes medication is needed because the problem requires more intervention or help from a medical doctor or psychiatrist who can work in conjunction with a therapist. This can be crucial and is discussed in the chapter on DEPRESSION DEFINITION AND TREATMENT.

One last note about searching for and asking questions of a therapist. When under stress from depression, anxiety, or any other challenge you will have difficulty searching and asking the questions discussed here. It is imperative that you don't wait until your symptoms are so severe that you have trouble coping with life and therefore struggle to find a counselor and ask the above questions. You may need someone to do this for you. There is more information on this subject in the chapter titled, HOW TO FIND A THERAPIST OR COUNSELOR. Good luck.

chapter eight

HOW TO FIND A THERAPIST OR COUNSELOR

This chapter is a duplicate of the last chapter in book 1. I repeat it in this book for those who chose not to buy that book.

How to Find a Therapist or Counselor

If you have health insurance with mental health coverage, then contact them for a list of mental health providers they will allow you to see. You may want to check with your primary care physician who may be familiar with therapists accepted by your insurance, which he or she trusts. Potentially your insurance company may not have the therapist you want to work with on their list of providers. In such cases you may have to pay for all your therapy if you choose to go to a therapist who is out of network, meaning not on your insurance company's provider list. You may very well have a mental health phone number to call for preauthorization on the reverse side of your insurance card. Some insurance companies provide members with a booklet which lists mental health providers in your area. Other insurances may only provide a list on the Internet, which you can download to your computer. You should inquire if a preauthorization is required prior to making an appointment. If you are able to preauthorize your first appointment, the chances of having to pay the entire fee will be reduced.

Before you start contacting prospective providers, please be aware that most insurance companies will not pay for marriage counseling. They will usually only pay their part of the fee if you are given a mental health diagnosis after an evaluation with a counselor. A diagnosis would be such conditions as depression, anxiety, obsessive compulsive disorder, post-traumatic stress disorder or any of many other diagnoses found in a manual called the DSM-V. This is the Diagnostic and Statistical Manual for Mental Disorders. Every mental health professional should have this manual because it lists all the mental health disorders people experience. Your insurance carrier will have their own specific rules regarding what types of diagnoses they are willing to cover. It might be helpful when you first call the insurance company to tell them generally why you are seeking counseling so they can tell you if your counseling will be covered. This may be uncomfortable for some people and unfortunately this might prevent them from seeking help. You will never see these insurance representatives and they will not know you so don't let this stop you. Most of the people you will talk to will not be in your city or state. The insurance company will almost always say that the conversation with you is not a guarantee of coverage. This can be a little tricky so be smart and take notes.

Some insurance companies do not have lists of providers, so you can go to anyone you like. Depending on the coverage your company has, you may be responsible for a small co-pay or for 50% or more of the fees for counseling. Ask who you can see and what fees you are responsible for when you call the mental health preauthorization number on your insurance card. If they allow you to see anyone you choose then it may be up to you to find a counselor because they might not have a provider list. There are some insurance plans that require you to only go to their facility where they have counselors on staff. The bottom line here is that if you have insurance and you want to go to a certain counselor, the chances are insurance may not pay for you to see him or her. In order to see the counselor of your choice you may need to pay the fees yourself. This is where negotiating for payments that fit your ability to pay can be very important. Don't be afraid to ask about this!

If you are on your own to find a counselor, you can look in the phone book for counselors or do a search online for the same in your area. You can search for clinical social workers, psychologists, and marriage and family therapists to see what comes up. Some states have lists of these same professionals in their department of professional licensing, so you can try that kind of a search also. This would assure that you are seeing someone who is licensed. You can also try looking on national registers for these professions. "Find a Psychologist," is a website that is helpful; there are also several registers such as The National Association of Social Workers, The American Board of Examiners in Clinical Social Work, The American Psychological Association, and The Association for Marriage and Family Therapy. These are all good places to start.

Authorizing Evaluations and Therapy Sessions

As mentioned above, you will need to call your insurance's mental health authorization line to receive permission to see a therapist. You may be given an authorization number to take with you to the first appointment. If this is the case, make sure you write it down and take it with you. Many insurance companies will authorize from two to six sessions initially for an evaluation and follow up appointments. Some insurance companies may authorize only an initial evaluation and will require the therapist to contact them for additional sessions after reviewing the diagnosis and treatment plan. Some plans, depending on the type of insurance package you have, may authorize from as little as three to as many as 20 or more sessions per year, per incidence of the same diagnosis. If this is the case, they may require the therapist to submit the progress notes and/or updated treatment plans at certain predetermined points along the way. If you max out the total sessions allowed, they might require the therapist to submit reasons why therapy should go beyond the maximum along with another treatment plan, if it is necessary. If they will not pay beyond this limit you may have to pay for the remaining appointments.

What Kind of Counseling Will Insurance Companies Pay for?

As indicated earlier, insurance companies will pay for patients to see a counselor if they have a diagnosis like depression or anxiety and others, but most do not pay for marriage counseling. Very often, however, in my experience as a therapist, at least one or both of the spouses who are seeking therapy have symptoms of depression or other mental-emotional conditions that may qualify for a diagnosis the insurance company will accept for payment. This is why it is important to diagnose both spouses when they come for treatment. If a qualifying diagnosis is made for either spouse, treatment may require individual therapy as well as marriage therapy because the marriage may be the cause of the diagnosis of depression, etc. It is up to the therapist to decide what to do in terms of a treatment plan. So even though insurance companies do not pay for marriage counseling directly, they will pay for the treatment of depression, anxiety, etc. and part of the resulting treatment may be marriage counseling.

Employee Assistance Programs

A note about Employee Assistant Plans or EAP as they are called. They are also referred to as Employee Assistant Programs. These are programs some companies provide their employees and their families. They receive professional help for individual therapy, marriage therapy, or any diagnoses, regardless of what they are. Sometimes employees are referred to these resources to avoid disciplinary measures or as a method of helping a problem at home or work from getting out of control, thus avoiding disciplinary action or termination. Some companies require updates to the immediate supervisor of the employee and other companies turn a blind eye and don't want to meddle in what is being done, especially if the treatment has nothing to do with work performance. This is a great way to get help for your family if your employer offers it. These programs will usually offer from two to eight sessions free of charge. You can check this out by contacting your Human Resources office. If you need therapy beyond the allowed number you will be referred back to your mental health benefits through your insurance plan.

What to Ask When Shopping for a Counselor

The next step is calling and asking questions to determine who you will make an appointment with. As with any profession or business, you can find poor, fair, good, great, or excellent people in counseling. When you are looking for a doctor, you ask a lot of questions before you chose one. The same holds true for counselors; ask around about who have good reputations before making an appointment. Inquiring about their years of experience, specialties, and ages they serve are all important questions to ask when choosing a therapist. As you ask around you may be surprised how many of your acquaintances know counselors. Don't be afraid to ask; there is nothing to lose unless you are the type who would rather lose your family, child, marriage, or sanity rather than your pride. By the time you need help, many of the people in your world are probably aware something is wrong, and if they are real friends they will want to help.

What Not to Ask

Early in my career, I received a phone call from a potential client who asked me questions about my experience, and he eventually said he wanted someone who had at least eight children and had been practicing for 20 years. I wanted to say, "What if the person you are describing has the children and the 20 years but is a lousy therapist?" I did say don't limit yourself with a therapist by placing prerequisites about his or her life experiences. He did not come in, and I would guess he had an adventure finding the right counselor for the job. I even talked to a woman one time who said her husband would not see a therapist unless he had been in the Vietnam War and had the same experiences in combat as he had. He believed no one could help him unless that person had been through the same experiences. The truth is, no one we go to will ever have the same experiences we have, so if that is our philosophy, we will be out of luck. The point being, if we **want** to change, there is someone out there who can help us with those changes. We do need a counselor who will listen and understand us. Without this quality we will have no confidence in him or her and will probably not go back. If the therapist allows us to share our inner-self and we sense that he or she is truly trying to understand, we will feel a sense of relief and will start to trust. This is how a positive client/therapist relationship will develop. If a therapist jumps in and starts giving direction and advice without establishing a relationship then most likely the client will feel just as misunderstood in that setting as he or she does in the world outside therapy. This is unfortunate because the client may get the message that counseling does not work.

If you have a poor experience in therapy, give someone else a try just as you would with a doctor. You may have had a less than positive exam with a doctor, but I hope you did not give up and instead found someone else you are comfortable with. I ask you to think the same way with counselors. A study was done some years ago to determine what the most important factors were in positive outcomes in counseling. They discovered the most important factors were, in order: the motivation of the client, the relationship with the therapist, and then the type of therapy that was used. Hopefully this has been helpful when you are in need of a counselor.

chapter nine

MARRIAGE COUNSELING: WHAT IS IT LIKE?

Do Insurance Companies Pay for Marriage Counseling?

Here is the big problem with marriage counseling. Most insurance companies will not pay for it or they may pay for only a portion of it. This dilemma can be overcome if either of the spouses have a diagnosis such as depression, which has been caused by the deteriorating marriage. If a legitimate diagnosis of depression or other disorder is made by the counselor and is the identified cause for treatment then marriage counseling may be utilized as one of the modes of treatment for the depression, etc. This happens in my practice because there are some really damaged people who come in with difficult marriage relationships that have worn them down over time. Therefore, when you go into the counselor if you think you or your spouse is suffering from something more than just irritation, you may need treatment along with the marriage counseling. Also, if you do have an EAP (Employee Assistance Program) through your employment then you can receive marriage counseling free of charge because marriage counseling is offered within the scope of many of these programs. They are usually limited in number from one to eight sessions.

There are some programs, depending on where you live, that may subsidize your marriage counseling. Check with your religious leader if you have one because many do have training in marriage counseling. Religious leaders may be willing to help you pay to get such therapy and many religious-based organizations have social service programs that might be able to help you get what you need. Be bold and ask around; you may be very surprised by what you find. If you have Medicaid you can go the local Mental Health Clinic and they will be able to help you.

Before you decide you cannot afford marriage counseling you need to read the chapter in this book regarding the COSTS OF GOING TO A COUNSELOR VERSUS NOT GOING. Please do this! The previous chapter, HOW TO FIND A THERAPIST OR COUNSELOR is another chapter that may be helpful to you.

What Happens When You Go into the Counselor's Office

After identifying a marriage counselor and making an appointment, here is what you will probably do when you enter the office. You will be asked to fill out information about your name, address, phone numbers, employment, insurance, fees or co pays, and what you hope to accomplish in marriage counseling. You may also be asked to sign an arbitration agreement in some larger outpatient counseling/treatment centers that have affiliation with medical centers. This means if you are unsatisfied with the therapy you will not sue but your case will be sent to an arbitrator or a third party who will decide if your complaint is serious enough to require some sort of compensation for you. You may also be asked to sign an agreement that if you plan on hurting yourself, someone else, or property you will call the therapist instead.

Finances

Prior to going into the appointment, you will be asked how the fee will be paid and if you have insurance what portion it covers. If you do not have insurance then you may be asked for payment up front or arrangement for monthly payments will be discussed. If you are going to pay out of pocket you should ask if they will charge you less per session.

Meeting the Counselor/Therapist

Marriage counselors have many different ways of approaching this important task; their methods of counseling may not work for every couple. The following is a typical approach I take when meeting with couples but it does not always apply because of different circumstances. I also want to make it very clear that I never, ever take the approach of blaming one or the other in marriage counseling. This approach does not work, in my opinion, because if you start blaming, the person who is blamed will leave and never return. I also believe that by teaching the principles and ideas in this example, couples can learn how to resolve their problems effectively. This avoids the blame game and, hopefully, they won't need me again because they will have the skills to resolve their marriage concerns.

When meeting the clients for the first time I look over the application form and what they want to accomplish. I ask each person to tell me what their impression of the marriage is now and if they could change anything what would it be. After getting a good understanding of each side from both spouses, I meet with each person individually. This is helpful because I hear what each person could not say with the other in the room. The picture becomes clearer after these brief interviews and, depending on what I sense from both people, I ask if they think there are some mental health issues they need to deal with individually first before we start marriage counseling.

The following is a list of roadblocks to enhancing a marriage or any relationship I give to couples as we decide if we need to resolve some personal issues prior to working on the marriage. Obviously, if someone is experiencing depression, for example, he or she will have difficulty giving his or her best effort in marriage counseling.

81

Roadblocks to Enhancing Marriage or Any Relationship

• Lack of motivation or desire to resolve conflicts by one or possibly both partners. This has a tendency to change from time to time for various reasons.

• Individual pathology. (i.e., depression, low self-esteem, perfectionism, personality disorders, drug or alcohol abuse, psychosis or any form of mental disorder)

• Situational stress. (i.e., death of a family member, loss of job, significant changes, rebellious child, etc.)

• Long or short-term conflicts in family resulting in lack of trust in spouse, little hope for reconciliation, pride etc.

• Physical/medical problems, which can be formidable barriers.

• Conflicts arising from being a victim of child abuse (i.e., sexual, physical, emotional, children of alcoholic parents, etc.) this includes battered wives and wives in current marriages unable to trust their present spouses even though they may not be abusive.

• The inability to give or take in any marriage relationship after being hurt in earlier life and relationships.

• Unwillingness to admit to mistakes and say I am sorry.

Infidelity.

• Any other reason for a person's inability or unwillingness to work at their relationships.

If I sense there are other individual problems, I meet with them together and request more information by asking questions about my impressions. I may request that both spouses fill out questionnaires to determine if there is a possible roadblock which needs to be addressed.

Motivation to Work on the Problems at Hand

I always ask the couple how motivated they are to resolve their problems on a scale from 0 to 10, 10 being the highest. You will note I discussed this at length in a previous chapter. Knowing this helps me to understand realistically what I am up against. I make it very clear to them that they need to be completely honest about this; however, experience has taught me that some individuals have made up their mind to divorce and coming to marriage counseling is an attempt to make it appear as if they are really trying to make it work, when all they are doing is putting on a show for others so later on they can say they did all they could but counseling didn't work. This is why I ask for honesty; I don't want to be deceived when the other spouse and I are giving our best efforts in vain.

Marriage Counseling is Education

At this point I tell couples that I need to educate them about some basic principles. This is why couples get marriage counseling: because they want to know how to have a successful marriage.

One side note before we continue. In order to get an unwilling spouse to come in, which is usually but not always a male, I tell the willing spouse that my approach to marriage counseling is the same as if you were going to get information about how to invest your money wisely, how to lay ceramic tile, or any other skill you want to acquire. Many of us go to seminars, conventions, and take webinars on the internet. These are all methods to educate us on almost any subject. The same goes with marriage counseling. It is an educational experience to teach people how to communicate and problem solve, etc. Talking to your unmotivated spouse in these terms may help him or her to consider going to counseling with you.

Now that I know what the problems are from our first interview I can teach a couple how to resolve them through tutoring and some practice. I now give them a handout I call,

How Marriages/Relationships May Be Enhanced

We must first understand the Differences between Men and Women

Women are:	Men are:
• Intuitive	• Concrete
• Right-brained	• Left-brained
• Multi-taskers	• Do one thing at a time
• Expect men to pick up on hints	• Don't get hints

I explain that men have only one program running in their computer at a time. These programs might be eat, sleep, work, watch TV, and so on. Each of their programs is neatly stored in a container which is completely isolated and insulated from all other programs. If one gets some kind of glitch in it he simply puts it back in its place and does not think about it. For example, a woman will sometimes say to her husband, "Doesn't this or that bother you?" And he says "No, why should it?" The reason is because it is stored away and he chooses not to think about it. Women, on the other hand, have a harder time compartmentalizing these thoughts. They can run more than one program at a time and are so conscientious that they cannot justify watching TV unless they are ironing or doing something else at the same time to avoid a feeling of guilt for taking some time out from their daily responsibilities. Their programs are in a different kind of storage container. It is like a snow globe, which you shake up at Christmas time and it appears as if it is snowing. These little flakes are programs floating around in a woman's head, and they are all connected through the liquid. If one of these programs gets a glitch in it, it turns the liquid dark and makes all the other programs dark as well. For example, if something does not go quite right at work or with her children it is easy for her to start thinking negatively. They don't like me at work or I don't spend enough time with my children. My husband doesn't pay attention to me and look at my hair, no wonder he doesn't love me like he used to. The meals I fix are not up to par and my house is such a mess. For women everything is related. One area of their lives affects all the other areas of their lives. This is why they can multitask, running the many aspects of a household and children's busy lives. This relatedness can be helpful and hurtful to their adjustments in life at the same time. Get the picture?

Now that we understand how differently we think as men and women, I talk about other differences we have which seem to get in the way of our relationships.

Add to This These Differences...

+ Family Background Differences

+ Individual Differences

+ Different Values

+ Different Dictionaries/Understandings

= Different Patterns of Behavior/Habits, or what I call...

Your Own Personal Style

I now explain that both husband and wife have different family backgrounds including how to discipline children, what kind of meals we eat and when, how we celebrate holidays and many other traditions and practices. We also have individual differences including food, dress, the type of cars we like to drive, and the list goes on and on. Two people can also have very different values even if they grow up in the same neighborhood. One person might be very religious and the other is not. One might think it's okay to use drugs and the other does not. One might think it's okay to spank a child and the other would never do that. We also have different dictionaries in our minds and interpret what we hear and see based upon those dictionaries and understandings. I was married 11 years before I knew what my wife meant when she said, "I'm fine." I thought that meant she was good and one day she finally told me what she really meant. Her definition of fine was, "I am not happy." That was a shock to me as I finally realized why I was in trouble so often.

All these differences add up to different patterns of behavior or habits. I call these patterns personal styles. I believe most people have one personal style or possibly two. This personal style is something we do every day, all day and at work, at home, or at play.

Two Kinds of Patterns/Habits

1. Personal Style

One spouse is a perfectionist, the other is easy-going. They decide to go on a road trip. What do you think the perfectionist will want to do prior to the trip? What do you think the easy-going person will do prior to the trip? There are many individualized personal styles and we all have one or two. This is the behavior we all fall back on every day in our lives and especially when stress enters the picture.

In the example above the perfectionist wants to have reservations, an itinerary, a map, and a list of things to pack days before they leave. The easy-going person says, let's not worry about this; let's just pack before we leave and we can find hotels along the way. Let's just go have fun. Can the perfectionist do that? If you sit and think for a moment you will be able to pinpoint your personal style as well as your spouse and your children. This is often their most prominent personality trait.

2. The Inability to Listen

This usually involves preparing a counter argument, instead of listening, while the other person is talking. This is a standard feature most of us receive at birth.

These two patterns prevent us from discussing or solving almost any issue. We can change this if we replace these patterns with effective ones.

With all these differences it is astounding to me that men and women stay together as long as they do. With this in mind, how do we change these patterns to understand each other and solve problems? First of all, we don't have to change each other; we just have to desire to change the way we communicate and problem solve, with a few other ideas thrown in.

Six Steps to Change Your Pattern

1. Communication

There Are Two Parts to Communication: sending and receiving.

Sending	Receiving
I feel (a feeling word goes here i.e. happy, sad, misunderstood, etc.) About (describe, be specific) Because (your motives, goals & values)	Restate/paraphrase/or say in your own words what the sender said until he or she believes that you understand

The receiver repeats back to the sender what he or she heard, until the sender is satisfied that he or she has understood the message. You must include the feeling word because it is vital in communication. When this is done they switch roles.

Let me give you a real example of how this works. I had worked with a very sharp couple who were foster parents and did a very good job with a couple of difficult teenage boys. They hadn't taken in a foster child for some time and one day the wife called me, asking if they could come and see me. I was happy because I thought they were going to request another foster child. When they sat down in my office, I asked how I could help and she said, "If he doesn't change, I want a divorce." After listening to them for a while I gave them this handout and taught them how to communicate using the format above. I asked who wanted to go first and she said immediately, "I do." I told the husband to listen carefully because he would have to say back to her in his own words what she was about to say. She started out with a statement something like this. "I am hurt and angry about every time we sit down to discuss important matters with the children because no sooner do we get started and you get up and walk away and it makes me feel like you don't care about me and the children." I then told the husband to repeat back to her what she just said and he said. "You're angry and upset with me because when we sit down to deal with the children I get up and leave, making you feel like I don't care about you or the kids." She said, "That's right." I told him it was his turn to tell her what he was feeling and thinking, using the same format. He said, "I feel inferior to you about dealing with the kids because you have a degree in child development and you are so much better at this than me because I am just a janitor." I looked at her and she was shocked. I asked her to pick her jaw off the floor and repeat back to him what he had said. She said, "You feel inadequate about talking to the kids because I have a degree and you believe you don't have anything to offer because you are a janitor." He said, "Yes, I have always felt that way."

Before they communicated with each other using this format I could feel the tension in the air between them. After they shared their feelings and understood each other the entire atmosphere of the room completely changed. There is something about sharing our feelings that softens what we say to each other and brings understanding. When this happens both people feel understood and validated. Remember this, **when communicating we do so to understand, not to agree! This first step does not solve problems, it brings understanding and insight.** After I have worked with a couple for a few sessions and we work on this skill and I know they have the process down, we graduate to step two called, No Lose Problem-Solving.

2. No Lose Problem-Solving

State the Problem/List All Possible Alternatives/Check Off the Options You Can Live with.

After we have identified a problem which needs to be resolved, I teach the couple No Lose Problem-Solving, (From P.E.T. In Action, by Dr. Thomas Gordon) which is discussed in the chapter entitled, A BRIEF EXAMPLE OF A PARENTING COURSE. Rather than explaining the process again in this chapter I would encourage you to review No Lose Problem-Solving in that chapter.

An example of No Lose Problems Solving for a Marriage Problem

This example is of one spouse who wanted a couch and the other who wanted a television.

Do we buy a couch or a TV?

- Buy a couch this year and get a television next year
- Buy a couch from Goodwill and buy a used television from a pawn shop
- Buy a couch this year and borrow a better television from parents now
- Buy a couch now with 90 days same as cash and do the same with a television
- Buy a couch now with 90 days same as cash and buy a television on credit for a year
- Buy a couch now with a credit card and buy a television now
- Buy them both on one-year credit
- Buy a television now with 90 days same as cash and buy a couch on credit for a year
- Buy a television now with a credit card and buy a couch now
- Buy a television from a pawn shop and buy a couch this year
- Buy a television this year and get a couch next year

In marriage and other areas of life we have difficulty resolving problems when we think in terms of "I am right and you are wrong." "My ideas are better than yours." Instead, we need to think Win/ Win as Stephen R. Covey suggests when going into any negotiation. When finished with this exercise there were a number of alternatives both spouses checked, and they decided on a solution without disagreement. At this point in therapy we start taking each issue in the marriage using this skill, and by the time we have resolved two or three problems the couple has this process down.

Specific Marriage Agreements/Contracts

In most cases of marriage counseling I create with the couples a number of marriage agreements targeted specifically at preventing reoccurring problems from arising. For example, if there is a lack of trust between a wife and husband because of infidelity, one of the first agreements we would come up with is that the spouse who has been unfaithful will never be alone with a member of the opposite sex. If a situation arises where he or she can't prevent such a circumstance as in a work-related assignment, then the agreement is that he or she will immediately and call the spouse to inform them of the situation. They will then decide how they will handle it. If one spouse wants to be reassured regarding the love his or her companion has for him or her, we have drawn up agreements that the other spouse will not leave home without saying, "I love you." We may also indicate how many times a day they would both feel comfortable saying they love each other. All kinds of specific agreements can be created, agreed-upon and when this is done both persons sign the document, making it a contract.

Dating

Every week a date is required to work on the romance. A fire needs logs to continue to burn and produce heat. The same goes with love. Just because we have been together or been married for some time does not mean that dating isn't necessary. It Is Vital.

Some years ago, I started asking couples when they last went on a date with each other. I was shocked to hear their responses. Most couples said that they do not recall the last time they went on a date together. Nowadays I am shocked if anyone says they date, but it does happen. Dating is critical in the marriage and should never, ever stop. My counsel to every couple is to pick out a day or evening each week for a date and make it a habit without exception. I understand at times other things may get in the way; however, if this happens then they need to decide how they're going to make up that date, hopefully the next day. If you plan this I promise it will pay off in tremendous dividends for the relationship. I also recommend getting out of town for an overnight romantic getaway once a quarter. Even if all you can do is to find someone to take care of the children and be home alone that night. Husbands, step up and make this happen. If you insist, it is more likely to take place and you will be happy with the results.

Another thing that helps with dating is to rotate from week to week who has responsibility for getting the babysitter and deciding where to go on the date. It does not have to be costly. It can be very simple; be creative and this can make a major difference in your marriage. The important thing is to focus on each other and the relationship.

Share Equally the Responsibilities in the Home

It doesn't matter whether the wife is working outside the home or not. If she is a homemaker she is working full time, 24 hours each day, seven days a week. She, or if it happens to be a he, has no breaks or lunch hours. Try working that kind of schedule, with children no less. It can be brutal dealing with those kids because they are always in need of something and it never stops.

It never ceases to amaze me how some men think they can come home from work and sit down and do nothing except watch television. They won't help with dinner, the kid's homework, getting the kids ready for bed, baths, etc. because they have worked hard all day. What do they think their wife has been doing all day and when did she get to sit down and do nothing? As I previously stated, it does not matter whether she works outside the home or not, it is unfair for her to have to continue working until she collapses when all the kids are asleep. Then later on when he is finished watching television, the husband wonders why she doesn't want to be intimate. She asks for help but has given up sometimes years before because she always gets the same answer that he has the right to rest from his labors because in his mind he works harder than her. She has stopped asking because she knows he won't help and, in fact, he may ridicule her. Therefore, she is tired, frustrated, and, in many cases, angry that he won't help. They are his children as well as her children and this is not fair. Fair is for both spouses to work together to take care of the meal, dishes, homework, discipline, baths, and tucking the kids into bed. When this is all done they can both sit down and have some down time together. How much more likely is the wife in this last scenario to be in the mood for intimacy than in the first example?

Men if you went to work and someone else was only doing part of their job and slacking the rest of the time, how would you feel toward that person? You are irritated at first then you become resentful and eventually you might jump to angry. Why would your wife be any different? Do you get my point? I have said this in another chapter in this book but it is worth repeating here. When a wife finally decides that she can be a single parent more easily than being a married parent, because her husband is just one more kid to pick up after, that is when divorce happens. Be fair with each other and share the responsibilities in the home equally, such that you both sit down at the same time every evening when everything is done. That is a marriage, a partnership, which leads to longevity, mutual respect, intimacy, and love.

Scheduling

Sitting down together and scheduling the upcoming events, once a week can make a huge difference, especially for the woman. (Just ask her)

This is not as important to men as it is to women, but believe me it will make a huge difference in your marriage. When the wife knows what to expect in terms of schedules, work, school activities, sports practices, games, etc. and how all of these activities are going to be accomplished, it will greatly reduce her stress and anxiety. Men, step up and see that you make sure this is done and if you do your wife will appreciate you, and this will be to your advantage.

Finances

Even though finances are listed last here it does not mean it comes last in marriage. Dave Ramsey says that 50% of divorces involve money problems. I believe we all need help with finances and I recommend to every couple that they take a course called Financial Peace University. This is an incredible nine-week course that teaches how to pay off debt, stay out of debt, establish an emergency fund, save/invest, and then give back when you are in a position to do so. You can find a local class by going to his website at www.daveramsey.com. Mr. Ramsey has a bestselling book called, "The Total Money Makeover," everyone should have a copy of this book. Being on the same page with money is crucial in a marriage and adopting Dave Ramsey's methods is the best way I have ever seen to do it. Don't let differences in the way you deal with money sabotage your marriage. Find where to take this course and go!

These are the skills I teach to couples, and I believe if every couple worked at them we would see fewer divorces, stronger marriages, and happier families. These are not hard skills to master, and if you are consistent in applying them, your children will pick up on these same skills and their marriages will be much more effective and strong. How gratifying it is to look at your children when they are married and to see that they are demonstrating the positive traits you taught them through your example.

A Very Important Handout

I often give a handout to couples during marriage counseling and I believe all married couples would be much better off if they would discuss this one page of information in detail. The document is called, "The Paths Through Conflict," from a book called, *Do I Have to Give Up Me to Be Loved by You,* by Jordan Paul Ph.D and Margaret Paul Ph.D. In essence, the handout briefly summarizes what the book describes in detail - what happens when conflict arises in marriage. We can take one of two paths: protection or evolution. The path of protection is defensive and closed to learning or understanding the other person. On this path we avoid responsibility for our feelings and behaviors as well as the consequences they cause. We either comply with our spouse, attempt to control him or her, or we become in-different. When the marriage takes this direction, the consequences are negative causing distance and lack of love. If we take the path of evolution which is not defensive but open, we assume personal re-sponsibility for our feelings, behavior and consequences. This leads to learning about ourselves and our spouse. We begin to explore by being open to being affected by the other even though it might cause fear and pain. We also will accept that there are good reasons for our feelings and our spouse's feelings. Some of the areas we become open to explore are our childhood, our fears, our beliefs, etc. The end of this path takes us to more intimate love and an evolving relationship with personal freedom and resolution of conflicts.

When discussing these concepts, I find that couples can see their own feelings and behaviors more objectively. As they read each section they are less likely to become defensive and are more willing to consider their own behaviors. The book goes into detail about each area described and there is much more that couples will find valuable in the book as they work on their marriages. I recommend this book to any couple who wants to improve their marriage. Get the book, read it, study it, and apply it.

Finally

It is very interesting to me in marriage counseling how when a couple gets to the point at which they are communicating effectively, problem solving, dating regularly, sharing responsibilities equally, scheduling, and on the same page financially, we come to a conclusion as a team that they don't need to come back. This is the time I most look forward to when they say, "we don't need you anymore". Folks, this is not difficult to do; if you need help go get it. Learn how to do these things and your marriage can be successful, if you both want it badly enough.

chapter ten
MARRIAGE COUNSELING: IT TAKES TWO

Let's discuss what motivates couples to get help.

Motivation to See a Marriage Counselor: The Main Ingredient

Before this happens, there is usually a crisis in the marriage which motivates either one or both partners to consider getting help. It is always better if a couple decides to get help without a crisis motivating them; good outcomes result from those who simply want to enhance their marriage. In most of these cases both are equally motivated and love each other. This is the ideal which, unfortunately, is not the most common circumstance. In the majority of cases I see, one spouse is more motivated than the other. This can change back and forth for several reasons. For any therapist the hope is that both spouses are motivated when they are seen. The following are different descriptions of how this motivation changes.

The Motivated Spouse and Unmotivated Spouse

I see many marriages where one spouse has given his or her all, trying with futility to improve the relationship. Over time, if the other does not respond then that person begins to become discouraged, depressed, and he or she begins to give up. Some either go on in the marriage with feelings of hopelessness or they just accept their lot and believe they must carry on for the good of the children in an unful-filled marriage. This person has done everything from reading books on relationships and marriage to talking with friends and relatives. They attempt to involve their partner in concepts and suggestions they get from books or others. They frequently do this with little or no success. They might even seek counseling either from a religious leader or a professional counselor. They often go alone because their efforts to get their spouse or significant other to go along have been met with no success and often negative comments. Some of these statements come in the form of, "You need help, not me" or "I hope they can fix you." The unmotivated person may actually go for a session or two in order to prove to the therapist that he or she is the normal one and to make it clear that he or she has no problems and that it is the other who needs fixing. This is especially true with people who have certain personality disorders discussed in the chapter on PERSONALITY DISORDERS in Book 1 and further on in this chapter. You really need to read that chapter!

Let's use a hypothetical couple to explain my example. If the first person described above who wanted help first, (we will call her Jill) finally wants out and makes her wishes known that divorce is what she wants, it is amazing how the other (or second spouse, which we will call Jack) can quickly become motivated and desire to work things out. Suddenly, he wants to go to counseling. When this takes place, I see a number of different responses from the Jills or formerly motivated spouses. In some cases, it may be too late because she has no more desire or motivation to work on the relationship and her decision to end the relationship is firm. On the other hand, she may tolerate going to a therapist for a time, or she might simply be worn out from all the months or years of trying and feels resentful and angry, or she may not care anymore. She may not be willing to go to counseling at all. She might finally decide to go after pressure is exerted upon her from friends and family as well as her husband Jack (who I call the formerly unmotivated spouse). It may even get to the point where Jill is considered the major problem by those who do not understand what she has been through. She might begin to feel resentful toward those who are applying pressure on her because she is burned out and doesn't have the emotional stamina to work on the relationship. This pressure can become very unfair and even ugly in its tone and intensity, especially if Jack, who now wants to work things out, plays the martyr card as if he is the victim and does not understand why Jill is sabotaging his efforts at reconciliation. I see significantly more women who want help in the beginning. Obviously, there are men out there who seek help first; however, my experience is that women are more likely to put forth the effort to get help, before most men. Sorry guys (those of you who don't get it) get your act together before it is too late -- women too, if this applies to you.

The Affair Trap

I need to throw in another real possibility here that happens often to begin an affair. That is the situation in which the spouse who becomes tired of trying begins to confide in another person of the opposite sex regarding his or her frustrations about his or her marriage. This can fan the flames of at least an emotional affair or even more problematic, the all-out affair. This starts innocently enough, but when this person starts to feel like he or she is really being listened to, maybe for the first time in years, it becomes very freeing emotionally. Those who experience this start sharing everything they have been holding in for so long and it feels wonderful to finally have someone who, at the time, is listening and validates their feelings. There we go with that all-important word, "validation." When this begins to happen outside the marriage relationship, then look out because it can lead to a bonding force that is hard to put the brakes on. This kind of relationship is how many affairs are born and grow into something we never imagined.

For those who become caught up into such relationships, be very cautious because you might find yourself falling for someone who may be listening now but who may be just looking for an opportunity, or they may be just as vulnerable. This sharing between two people happens so innocently that before you know it you are involved waist deep in an emotional or a physical affair.

To those who are the **unmotivated spouse**: You might want to think twice about not engaging with your spouse in marriage help because you never know who your spouse might be confiding in if you are physically and/or emotionally unavailable. If your spouse is asking or begging for your involvement, he or she is quite possibly saying, "If you don't have the desire to meet me in the middle and work on this then I am afraid I can't stay much longer." He or she may also be saying, "If you don't think our marriage is worth the effort, I know someone who does listen to me and does think I am worth their time."

In other words, <u>wake up if your spouse has been trying to get you to listen, or you may be in for the shock of your life. What has your spouse been saying to you lately?</u> Think about it!

Motivation to Divorce

I have found that when a wife gets to the point where she realizes that her husband is just another child she has to pick up after and serve, day in and day out, this is when she decides enough is enough. She effectively says, "I can do this a lot easier without him because I feel like his mother. He is just a child, and all he wants is a mother and a sex partner." This is when emotional divorce becomes established. The other spouse may be shocked and clueless why the other would suddenly want out. In his mind he was not told that things were this bad. He would have done something if he had only been told. In some cases, he is correct because the wife did not tell him directly. In other cases, he was told but would not listen, or he realized it was inevitable and had been coming for some time. There are numerous spouses out there who live in denial and don't want to hear what the other has to say. Some spouses feel marginalized, demeaned, and controlled. If this is the case with you, the time will come when the truth must be made known.

The Insincere Spouse

Another variation I see all too often is the unmotivated spouse going in for marriage counseling, even though he or she has decided (without telling anyone, so they appear sincere as if they really want to reconcile) to eventually leave the marriage so he or she can say to others, and himself or herself, "We tried counseling but it didn't work." Early in my career I had a number of people who said they wanted to reconcile their marriage problems only to discover they were flat out lying and had made their minds up to divorce before coming in for counseling, but they wanted to put on a show for the family and friends that they were really trying to make it work. Some of these individuals even had girlfriends or boyfriends on the side and were planning their future lives while pretending to be invested in therapy. This is so blatantly dishonest and is why I ask each spouse, in our first session, if they are being completely honest regarding their motivation. I ask each couple how motivated they are on a scale of 1 to 10. I speak of dishonesty and reemphasize as I meet with them individually the need to be completely open with me.

I must confess, after experiencing a string of these situations around 1985, I had a couple come in to see me who were both in at least their second marriage. I was so tired of working as hard as I could in therapy with couples who were pretenders that I really let this couple have it. They probably thought I was a raging lunatic because I went on about how I wasn't going to invest in helping them if they wouldn't engage honestly in working as hard as they could, if they really loved each other. I think I apologized to them; I hope I did. I don't recall what happened to them. I hope anyone who reads this thinks long and hard about his or her motivation to enter therapy and that he or she won't pull this kind of stuff on his or her spouse/partner and a marriage counselor. Be responsible and honest people!

For marriage counseling to work in most cases, both partners need to be motivated. If this is the case then learning how to live with and love each other really is possible.

The Influence of Others on Motivation

Picture, if you can, a railroad car sitting in the middle of a track. The car represents a person who is trying to decide if he or she wants to stay in a marriage or any other relationship. The weight of the car can be heavy depending on how much abuse, neglect, lack of love, mistrust, or infidelity the person has endured from his or her spouse. The more negative the input the more the car is filled with weight. The more positive experiences like love, communication, time spent together, etc, the less weight it has. There are two destinations; the track to the left represents distance and no desire to be in the relationship. The destination to the left represents the dissolution of the relationship. The destination on the right side represents a complete and full desire to stay in the relationship, to work at it and eventually unify. Whenever pressure is applied by anyone including the spouse, friends, family, clergy, or (hopefully not) the therapist, the result is a heavier car, which begins to move to the left. This pressure also causes the track to incline on the right-hand side, making it more difficult for the individual to get to the right side. Pressure from anyone reduces mental and emotional energy to invest in the relationship, and it can cause confusion and eventual despair. Therefore, it is critical for the person who is struggling with staying in the relationship to have the ability to step back, get some space, and seek some help to see things clearly and objectively.

This is especially hard for someone who is weak and tired, either emotionally, physically, or both. If we are talking about someone who has low self-esteem and needs reassurance, these people will have more difficulty thinking for themselves. They will be hard-pressed to not allow the opinions of others to affect what they do or feel.

We have all seen this in some form or other, either from personal experience or in the lives of others. Therefore, we must be cautious and encourage such people to get help and some appropriate distance from any coercion going on from a manipulative spouse or well-meaning friends or family. This can be in the form of tending their children while they have a few hours to get away, to making sure that we do not press upon them our own feelings, beliefs, and values. These people need space to begin to put together reasonable solutions to their dilemma. They may need a place to stay for a while or a weekend out of town. They cannot do this with people pushing and blaming with "shoulds" and "shouldn'ts," etc. It is important here that we do not mess with free will. We don't know all the circumstances and conditions they are struggling with. The best thing we can do is to express love and support for what they choose.

If you disagree, let me explain. When we were first born into this world we were given a precious gift. That gift is our free will to choose our path in life. This path may be constricted by virtue of where we are born and what country, religion, and freedoms we have. However, one thing we all do have to a greater or lesser extent is the ability to choose to do with our circumstances what our opportunities present. When we are controlled by others and are forced to do what others want, we start to feel anxious, then irritated, aggravated and then we become resentful, and if it does not stop we can become angry. We have all seen such scenarios when a person suddenly abandons a marriage, family, or employment to the amazement of everyone. This is usually due to the person feeling coerced with no choices because he or she is boxed in on all sides with no way out. Such people have expectations from every side from a spouse, family, friends and even their own values and beliefs that make them feel hopeless and the only way out is to escape. They abandon all they have believed in their entire lives in some cases.

We must allow these people the opportunity to stretch themselves and to grow and make some hard decisions, all the while loving and supporting them. The best thing we can do is to give encouragement and express faith that they will come to the best conclusion for themselves. There are always exceptions to this such as when that person is being abused, emotionally, physically, or in any other way. Then we have a responsibility to step in and avert disaster for those who are unable to protect themselves. If this is what is happening then, by all means, step in and do something to protect them.

Otherwise, as we give space, encouraging them to get objective, professional help, if necessary, then it becomes much easier for those people to begin to toss overboard the weight in their railroad car and begin to push it to the destination on the right, if that is what they choose. The truth is, if we a push them with pressure to reconcile before they are willing, we add weight to their car and make it that much more difficult for them to push it back in that direction.

Personalities That Don't Do Well in Marriages

I am not the first to say miracles can happen and couples can really change. In some instances when this happens it is because of an ultimatum or fear of losing the one they love. However, I'm going to make a statement here, which I have found to be accurate in most relationships. This is also found in another chapter in this book. I believe it is important enough to include it here also.

THE BEST PREDICTOR OF CURRENT BEHAVIOR IS PAST BEHAVIOR. THE BEST PREDICTOR OF FUTURE BEHAVIOR IS CURRENT BEHAVIOR. EXPECT THE EXPECTED. DON'T EXPECT THE UNEXPECTED.

If you are dealing with unacceptable behavior in a spouse, and you are lucid enough to know it probably won't change, then you may be dealing with a personality disorder.

Especially difficult is the marriage in which one of the individuals has a personality disorder. Educating the public about personality disorders is one of the most important reasons this book was written. It is important that you read the chapter titled, PERSONALITY DISORDERS, in Book 1 in order to understand what I am trying to express here. Understanding this concept might save you or someone you love from years of misunderstanding, pain, and difficulty. These people are very hard to live with because they blame others for their own difficulties in life and, in the process, they make others' feel guilty. IF YOU OR SOMEONE YOU LOVE FEELS MANIPULATED AND RESPONSIBLE FOR SOMEONE ELSE'S HAPPINESS, PLEASE REVIEW THAT CHAPTER. It will be very enlightening, and I hope freeing from guilt and confusion at the same time.

An Example of a Spouse with a Personality Disorder

Some husbands (and to a lesser degree wives) believe they are superior to their spouses and think they are childish, oversensitive, and plain stupid. If this is the case then the road can be long and difficult. These persons often have personality disorders and are very hard to be married to. They do not change their behavior or say they are sorry, and they expect others to make changes to meet their expectations.

Let me give you a real-life example of a spouse with a personality disorder. A young wife, 26 years of age, with no children and marriage of over two years makes an appointment with me after struggling in her marriage. She feels helpless and depressed and has tried everything she could possibly think of to make her husband happy. The only emotion her husband demonstrates is when he is angry and threatens to harm her dog. She tries to be as nice as she possibly can for months on end. Still his behavior does not change. He is distant, unfeeling, and spends most of his time when he is not at work with his friends or watching TV. He believes he is special and deserves to be treated as such. She asks for help around the home, which is met with comments like, "I work hard and deserve to relax in my home." "You don't appreciate me and what I do for us." He expects her to have dinner ready when he arrives from work, even though she works full-time herself. When she expresses any of her feelings he uses ridicule accusing her of being too emotional. She responds by feeling hurt, insignificant, unloved, disillusioned, and trapped.

The Case of the Marriage with One Spouse Who Has a Personality Disorder and the Other Spouse Who Does Something Really Stupid

There is another very curious set of circumstances I see all too often. That is the case in which one spouse has a personality disorder and seems quite normal to people outside the immediate family and he or she can even fool some of the extended family for a time. Behind the scenes, within the family, these people are tyrants and treat the children and their spouse with impossible expectations and constant demands. The children grow up thinking this is normal and the spouse begins to believe he or she is crazy because he or she can't ever meet the other's expectations. Let's use Jack and Jill again as examples. Over time, the spouse without the personality disorder (Jack) begins to feel alone, unloved, depressed, and he runs out of desire to give any more to the marriage. In order to cope, Jack being the victimized spouse attempts to check out his hopeless feelings by confiding in someone at work or in other social situations. The next thing you know, he becomes emotionally involved with a coworker or has an affair. When this is revealed, he becomes the person with the identifiable problem. He has made the obvious grand mistake and is persecuted by Jill, the spouse with the personality disorder. He is now seen as the bad guy who has done the unthinkable and betrayed the marriage vows. Jill's family spurns Jack and even his own family and friends may make him feel guilty to the point where it can get ugly.

No one knows what Jack had to put up with for many years. If we could see Jill's behaviors, we would understand what lead him to do something he never thought he was capable of. By explaining this I am not condoning anyone who goes outside the marriage for understanding and love. The point here is to make you aware of what happens in these situations behind the scenes which we do not see. Let me explain with another an example.

After playing basketball one evening, a friend asks me if I think he is a good person. I was shocked and replied that he was one of the nicest people I knew. Not only was he a great individual, but he was a very successful businessman with a wife and children and they had just built a new home. Soon after this discussion the stupid thing happened; the husband kissed a single woman in the neighborhood. To this point in time everyone believed this couple had an outstanding marriage. This news spread quickly, and everyone was taken aback because of how out of character it was for this man to do such a thing. The wife's reaction was swift and strong and a bit over the top and almost as surprising as the husband's behavior. She wanted everyone to shun her husband and punish him for this terrible thing he did. She wanted their church congregation to expel him, and when this did not happen she became angry with those in charge and viewed them as her enemies. Yes, the husband's behavior was inappropriate and was cause for her to lose trust in him. However, her reaction and then her behavior toward those who would not throw him to the wolves, so to speak, were almost as shocking as her husband's stupid behavior. She would not speak to anyone who would not spurn him. This was amazing to see as she literally would cross people off her list of friends who would not do as she required. They eventually divorced, and in a surprise move to everyone, the older children chose to live with their father. Eventually, one of the other children went to live with him also.

What others did not see was the way this wife and mother treated her family when others were not around. She was controlling, demanding, and critical within the family setting. The husband had been miserable for years along with the children. Over time, he started to look for some love and comfort he was not receiving in his marriage and did the thing that others would view as the obvious betrayal to the marriage. He was the identifiable bad guy. I am not condoning his behavior and never would, but I understood what lead him to act as he did.

This is something that happens on a daily basis around the world, when a spouse treats his or her family members so poorly that the other spouse finally does something he or she knows was wrong. The finger of blame is pointed at this person, and no one has a clue what he or she has been living with in the private confines of the home. My message here is to not judge the behavior of others when you do not know the entire story. There are always two sides to a story so don't get caught up defending or believing someone is bad if you don't know all the details of what goes on behind closed doors.

I have two other comments regarding spouses with personality disorders. When the decision to leave the marriage is made by the spouse without the personality disorder, the one with the disorder is frequently shocked that the other is not willing to continue on because of a sense of entitlement the personality disorder causes. People with personality disorders do not take personal responsibility for their behavior. To them it is always other people who have the problems.

It is common for a spouse with a personality disorder to accuse the other spouse of infidelity when he or she is the one who is unfaithful. This is called projection when someone accuses someone else of their own indiscretions.

Finding a Counselor

If you are at a point where you can't get your spouse to go to counseling with you, then you probably need to find a counselor for individual therapy. I address this in the chapter on HOW TO FIND A COUNSELOR OR THERAPIST. If you feel you need to talk to someone, you should review that chapter. Networking with others to find someone to go see is helpful. If money is an obstacle then it is time to ask for help from family, friends, or if you are affiliated with a church, from a pastor or priest. You have the ability to make this happen, get help, for your sake, and if you have children, for them too. If you have insurance, Medicaid, or Medicare then it will be easier to make this happen. Push forward and you will find someone to confide in who can help you determine what to do rationally and thoughtfully. There are therapists who will see you and accept reasonable monthly payments.

I have one word of caution here. You may run into therapists or clergy with agendas who don't really listen and therefore don't understand you, or who think you should stay in a relationship no matter what damage has been done. They may not understand the many subtle forms of abuse which can be occurring behind the scenes, or they may not believe the other person is doing anything wrong. This kind of counselor can have damaging effects on your free will and may heighten your guilt to do things you do not feel are in your best interests. Be careful and ask questions of people you trust who themselves have been to someone you might potentially go to see. Sometimes what you will need is to get stronger by getting individual therapy first to overcome depression, anxiety, and self-doubt until you are strong enough to make a decision from a position of personal strength. This happens frequently in my practice. Sometimes all a person needs is to feel good about himself or herself and then he or she is able to make choices about the future that were never thought possible weeks or days earlier.

chapter eleven

DOMESTIC ABUSE AND WOMEN'S SHELTERS

There are many women who are in abusive relationships whether married or not who stay in them because they believe they have no way out. Some are truly frightened because they have been threatened by the man/husband/boyfriend that if they leave or do anything counter to his will he will hurt them or even threaten to kill them. They may also be afraid for their children or other extended family members. Many women have no way to support themselves and believe they are stuck forever with no options to leave or a way to provide a living for their family. There are many other scenarios which could be cited including the fact that there are some men who are intimidated by women and believe they are also unable to disengage without very severe consequences. It is to these people who are caught in an environment similar to a prison that I wish to address.

Power and Control

To demonstrate how domestic violence occurs I am taking information from a handout called, "Power and Control Wheel," produced and distributed by the National Center on Domestic and Sexual Violence, 4612 Shoal Creek Blvd. Austin, Texas 78756.

The handout referred to is a wheel and one could start at any point on the wheel depending on where the abuse begins.

"The Power and Control Wheel"

Intimidation: Making her afraid by using looks, actions, and gestures. Smashing things. Destroying her property. Abusing pets. Displaying weapons.

Emotional Abuse: Putting her down. Making her feel bad about herself. Calling her names. Making her think she's crazy. Playing mind games. Humiliating her. Making her feel guilty.

Isolation: Controlling what she does, who she sees and talks to, what she reads, and where she goes. Limiting her outside involvement. Using jealousy to justify actions.

Minimizing, Denying, and Blaming: Making light of the abuse and not taking her concerns about it seriously. Saying the abuse didn't happen. Shifting responsibility for abusive behavior. Saying she caused it.

Using Children: Making her feel guilty about the children. Using the children to relay messages. Using visitation to harass her. Threatening to take the children away.

Economic Abuse: Preventing her from getting or keeping a job. Making her asked for money. Giving her an allowance. Taking her money. Not letting her know about or have access to family income.

Male Privilege: Treating her like a servant: making all the big decisions, acting like the "master of the castle," being the one to define men's and women's roles.

Coercion and Threats: Making and/or carrying out threats to do something to hurt her. Threatening to leave her, commit suicide, or report her to welfare. Making her drop charges. Making her do illegal things."

These tactics and others are very effective in keeping a woman afraid and controlled through the intimidation techniques described above. In addition, there is also physical and sexual assault that further terrifies her and keeps her from taking steps to leave the relationship. This is a very helpless position to be in, and far too many women are living this way.

What Can Be Done to Help?

The National Domestic Violence Hotline can offer help to connect to local resources in your community. The phone number is 1-800-799-SAFE (7233), TTY for the Deaf 1-800-787-3224."

I would like to expand what I said above by inserting this handout produced by the National Domestic Violence Hotline.

When Someone You Know Is Abused: Information for Family and Friends

Understanding why it might be difficult to leave an abusive relationship can help you identify ways to support your loved one.

Situational Factors

Financial dependence on the abuser

Lack of support system to assist victims in recognizing and escaping the abuse

Lack of community response in understanding and protecting victims

Threats by the abuser when the victim tries to separate, including threats to kill the victim, the children or other family members, and/or to commit suicide. Knowledge of women who were killed after separating from their abusers heightens this fear.

Psychological Factors

Emotional ties to the abuser. Abuse doesn't necessarily mean that feelings of love will automatically end. These feelings are typically reinforced by periods of time in which there is no abuse and their partner is loving, or at least civil.

• A belief that victims should understand their abuser and help them to stop their destructive behaviors.

• A belief in the value of holding the family together and putting this belief above their own personal pain, fear, etc. Victims may, also, feel pressure from family and religion.

• Feelings of personal incompetence and self-doubt that lead victims to believe that they must have a partner to survive, even if that person is abusive. Over time, many increasingly question their own value, judgment, capabilities, and attractiveness as the effects of abuse eat away at their self-esteem.

• Self-blame and the need to defend the abuser. Because abusers punished victims for their inability to act properly or to meet their expectations, victims often believe that they are, in part, responsible for the abuse.

• The belief that violence is a normal part of all relationships.

• A belief in the total power of the abuser to act on threats made.

The Reality of Leaving a Domestic Violence Relationship

Victims and survivors of domestic violence have trouble finding apartments because they may have poor credit, rental, and employment histories as a result of their abuse. Susan a. Reif and Lisa J. Krisher. 2000. "Subsidized Housing and the Unique Needs of Domestic Violence Victim." *Clearing House Review*. National Center on Poverty Law. Chicago, IL.

• In the 2002 report by the U.S. Conference of Mayors, 44% of the cities surveyed identified domestic violence as the primary cause of homelessness. The United States Conference of Mayors. 1999. *A Status Report on Hunger and Homelessness in America's Cities*, p.39.

• Batterers often use child custody as a forum for further abuse through harassing and retaliatory legal actions. "Report of the American Psychological Association Presidential Task Force on Violence and the Family." *Violence and the Family*, 40 (1996).

• Eighty percent of women who are stalked by former husbands are physically assaulted by that partner and 30% are sexually assaulted by that partner. Center for Policy Research, Stalking in America, July 1997.

How Can I Help?

• Be supportive and nonjudgmental. Listen to your friend or family member; what they need most is someone who will believe them.

• Acknowledge that they are in a difficult and scary situation. Let them know that the abuse is not their fault. Reassure them that nothing they did or did not do caused the abuse.

• Don't be afraid to express your concern for their safety.

• Help them create a safety plan. Read safety planning tips and discuss them with your friend.

• Be supportive when your friend or family member is feeling alone or mourning the loss of the relationship. This is a normal part of the healing process.

• Encourage them to participate in activities outside of the relationship in order to support healthy attachments and to reduce their isolation.

• Encourage them to talk to people who can provide help and guidance. Offer to accompany them to talk with other family and friends. Find a local domestic violence agency that provides counseling and/or support groups. If they need to go to the police, to court, or to see an attorney, suggest going with them for moral support.

• Don't try to rescue your friend or family member. The decision to leave the relationship is ultimately theirs. But you can help when they decide to reach out.

• Focus on your concerns for your friend instead of criticizing the abuser. Your friend may not be receptive to your help if she feels she has to defend why she is in the relationship.

You Can Make a Difference!

• Urge your members of Congress to support additional funding for domestic violence programs through the Violence against Women Act, the Victims of Crime Act Fund, and the Family Violence Prevention and Services Act.

• Work with policy advocacy groups, such as state coalitions against domestic violence, to influence your state legislature to pass progressive domestic violence laws and ensure that local programs receive funding for prevention and intervention services.

• Volunteer at a domestic violence shelter or make a donation to a local program.

• Serve as a language translator for domestic violence programs.

• Offer professional services such as legal services and tax preparations for survivors, fundraising, event planning, or other services for domestic violence programs.

• Educate your community and arrange speaking engagements at schools, churches, or civic groups to address the problems of domestic violence.

• Become a member of a local, state, or national domestic violence organization to learn more about what is happening in the effort to stop domestic violence in your community and country."

Please call the 24 hour National Domestic Violence Hotline at 1-800-799-SAFE (7233) or TTY 800-787-3224 to discuss your concerns and questions."

Help and Safety Are More Available Now Than Ever Before When Someone You Know Is a Victim of Domestic Violence

Reaching out for help at a domestic violence victim assistance center or women's shelter is much easier than ever before with many programs that can offer immediate protection and a place to stay which is safe from the violence. By calling the above hotline or contacting a local women's shelter, a woman can receive immediate crisis intervention and housing that protects her and her children from the abuser. Most of these shelters have 24-hour advocate support, with attorneys who volunteer to give legal advice, offering court and protective orders, stalking injunctions, and victim support. This means that calling or going to a shelter can give the victim and children immediate protection behind locked doors at a shelter and necessary court orders to place the law between them and the abuser. Counselors and crisis workers are there to meet with and give direction and protection options for the victims. The staff at these facilities is experienced in all the details and knows what victims have gone through as many of the staff and volunteers are former victims themselves. At many of these facilities there are numerous programs such as: rape recovery programs, child care centers, homeless housing assistance, parenting classes, children's self-esteem counseling and classes, individual counseling, rape education and prevention, medical services, access to donated clothing, and much more. There are also training programs available to help women receive an education or training so she can find a job and career. Childcare is often available to enable her to receive and attend these programs. There is someone waiting right now to talk to any victim of domestic violence and to provide them with safe haven. If you know someone involved in domestic violence help her to connect to these organizations and, if at all possible, see that she meets with them in person to enhance her connection and trust.

It takes courage and strength to go forward, and I believe you can do this. Go forward; make the calls and contacts and start your new life. You deserve it!

chapter twelve

A BRIEF EXAMPLE OF A
PARENTING COURSE

Below is a brief outline from, *Becoming a Better Parent Course,* which I used to teach and which is no longer in print, nor is it used today. The reason it is not used any more is not because the concepts are not useful; it is because other excellent courses were being offered elsewhere, and it was discontinued.

When education on parenting is needed by my clients, I teach them these concepts. Each of the principles below is followed by a brief discussion just as I do with my clients. My hope is to give you an idea of what you will learn when you sign up for a parenting course in your community.

Parenting Education, Every Parent Needs It

The reason every parent needs parent education is because every parent needs to learn how to be a therapist for his or her child or children. With good training and sound principles, you can not only become confident in your parenting skills, but you are with the child more than anyone and are therefore in a position to be the most helpful to him or her. Yes, there are situations where professional help and even hospitalization are required. However, I believe we could avoid many of the problems we face with our children if we all learned some basic parenting skills, which we did not get from our families as we grew up.

When children escalate to a point where their behavior is out of control, all the counseling in the world will not make a difference, unless the child wants help. I am amused by teachers and school administrators who dish out the advice that what that child needs is counseling. If the child is unwilling, counseling is essentially useless and one hour per week of therapy to change a lifetime of inappropriate behaviors is a tall order. There are three alternatives in these cases, the first being, let the child do whatever he or she wants and the consequences will follow. The second option is to teach the parents how to be therapists, which I think is the best option. The third is to send the child to a program for trouble youth, which is very expensive. This last option may work for some families who have the finances to utilize such programs. A web search for, "Troubled Youth," would be a good start for those who need significant help for a wayward child. Good research into these programs is vital before sending a child away, so make sure you ask questions of program representatives and ask for reviews from parents who have sent their children to their facilities. It would also be wise to check with state licensing departments to receive feedback regarding any program you are considering.

If you want to learn how to be a better parent and a therapist for your child, then pay attention. Most parenting courses are eight to 12 lessons once a week, so what I am giving you is a condensed, crash course.

The following concepts are divided into different categories. Some are concepts we need to understand; some are to be avoided and others are to be put into action as skills.

CONCEPT #1

Kids Talk in Code

This is something we need to understand.

This first concept is something all parents know about their children because our children don't know or don't understand what they are feeling; they just cut loose and say whatever comes out of their mouths. For parents, it is crucial to acknowledge their coded language and then help them by decoding their confusing messages so we can both understand what is going on. When we do this, we begin to establish a bond between ourselves and our children. We become a team through mutual understanding, and this builds love and respect between parent and child. Doing this makes the child feel understood and validated.

Illustration by Matt Anderson

When we, as parents, are trying to understand what a child is thinking, feeling, and doing we often feel frustrated because they express emotions in ways that don't make sense to us. Consequently, we have trouble knowing what they are feeling much of the time. Parents, whether we like it or not, we must try and DECODE what the child says. The way we decode is actually very simple. We pretend we are a large mirror and we reflect back to the child what he or she says. We do this by identifying their feelings and emotions and reflecting them back to the child, as depicted with this cartoon of the first concept. Decoding is explained in Concept #3.

An example of this process is the young teenager who comes home from school and says, "I hate orchestra and I'm going to quit."

CONCEPT #2

Avoid Using Communication Roadblocks

This is something we need to avoid.

The Parent's Usual Response is One of the Road Blocks to Communication:

- Commands and Orders

- Domination and Control

- Judgment and Criticism

- Permissiveness and Giving Up

Many of us, as parents, would respond immediately with one or more of the Roadblocks to Communication in concept #2. This first example would be Commands and Orders with a response like, "Oh no you're not; you're going right back tomorrow and you're going to like it! Next is Domination and Control. "I will tell you when you can quit or not, and you're going to play that instrument until we get our money's worth out of it. Do you know how expensive that was?" Judgment and Criticism is next. "You always give up before you finish anything; you don't appreciate anything we do for you." Last is Permissiveness and Giving Up. "I am tired of trying to help you to do everything; I give up."

Do you see how these communication roadblocks can damage the relationship we have with our children? Now let's go back to concept #1 and decode what the child has said about the orchestra incident. We do this with the next step in Concept #3.

CONCEPT # 3

What to do When the Child is Upset or How to Decode

This is something we need to put into use as a skill.

• **Reflect a Feeling**

• **Summarize the Important Information** (Listen to the child and summarize only until understanding is accomplished and only then do you use the next step)

• **Honest Encouragement**

The child says, "I hate orchestra and I'm going to quit." Now turn on your decoder by identifying feelings and emotions and reflecting them back to the child. The parent says, "So you're upset about something that happened in orchestra and you don't want to go back." Do you see how you are acting like a mirror and you are just bouncing or reflecting back in your own words what the child has said? You can even simply say what the child said, "So you hate orchestra and don't want to go back." When you do this the child knows that you are trying to understand what he or she is experiencing. If you get it right the child will tell you and if not, he or she will correct you and tell you again. When you get it right the child will say something like, "Ya." Then you know you are on the right track. The child will hopefully go on to explain why or how he or she feels. If he or she does not go into detail then we need to reflect and summarize again to see if we are getting closer to what the child is feeling and thinking. In this case the child responded this way. "I hate orchestra because the teacher put me back in the stupid second orchestra." We do the same thing again by being a mirror and restating what the child just said, but we add a feeling word before we summarize what they said. "So you are hurt, discouraged and embarrassed because you were put back in second orchestra." The child responds, "Ya, a lot of those kids have been in orchestra a year longer and some of them even have private lessons so it isn't fair; I can't compete with them." In this case the parent reflects one more time. "So, you feel disappointed and discouraged because you were placed back in second orchestra, and because many of the other students have been playing a lot longer than you and some even have lessons and it is hard to compete with them." The child says, "Yes." Now you know you have got it and so does the child. The child will feel a bond with you because they know you understand. I believe you can see how this builds bridges of trust between you and them.

You will note here that each time you keep trying to reflect back to the child his or her feelings, as well as describing the situation that you go one step deeper into understanding until you get to the real reason the child is so upset. Notice the major difference between using the roadblocks to communication and using the reflective listening?

The first time you try this you might get a strange look from your child who might wonder what has happened to his or her parents. My advice is when you start to utilize any of these methods you will learn in a parenting class that you tell your children what you are doing. Don't keep your methods secret. Tell your kids you are going to start doing something new to improve the family communication.

Now Don't Get Confused Here Because I am Going to Give You a Little Different Way of Doing Step #3.

You will note here that the format below is basically the same as steps #1 and #3 above, with more structure to help you as you get started doing this reflective listening (which is what this is called). Some parents may not need to use the following format because they can incorporate the first one above. For many parents it may be well to use the following outline and once you get the process down you can go to the one above.

The Parent Says...

You feel (a feeling word, like happy, sad, disappointed, discouraged, unhappy, etc.)

About or When (describe the child's behavior and be specific)

Because (try to describe your child's needs, motives, goals and values)

When the child is upset it is important that we, as parents, understand his or her feelings. They need to know we understand them. It is the same for adults to know that the person we are communicating with understands what we are feeling. For example, if we are trying to tell a family member or friend how frustrated we are that they are not listening, then the degree to which we are frustrated usually increases. However, when they listen and reflect how we feel, our trust in them grows and we feel relieved that they understand. We feel validated! How do you feel when you know they are not listening to you? It can be real hard to feel good about sharing anything with them if they are distracted or not interested in what we have to say. Same thing with kids!

Let me give an example from a book called, *How to Talk so Kids Will Listen and Listen so Kids Will Talk*, by Adele Faber and Elaine Mazlish. I am using this example because I am hoping those who read this book will either check the book out at the library or pick up a copy for their own library. This particular example is actually a cartoon in their book. I will quote the statements but do not include the cartoon. You will get the picture. Above the cartoon are two statements. The first says, "Instead of Denying the Feeling, Give the Feeling a Name." The example is an exchange between a daughter and her father and goes as follows. The daughter says, "My turtle is dead. He was alive this morning." Father says, "Now don't get so upset honey." Daughter is crying now; Father says, "Don't cry. It's only a turtle." Daughter reacts, "WAH! WAH!" Father responds with, "Stop that; I'll buy you another." Daughter comes back with, "I don't want another one!" Father replies, "Now you're being unreasonable!"

Below this first cartoon is a statement. "It's strange. When we urge a child to push a bad feeling away, however kindly, the child only seems to get more upset." The following is their example of giving the feeling a name with appropriate reflective listening.

The daughter says, "My turtle is dead. He was alive this morning." Father replies, "Oh no. What a shock!" Daughter says, "He was my friend." Father responds, "To lose a friend can hurt." Daughter says, "I taught him to do tricks." Father says, "You two had fun together." Daughter says, "I fed him every day." Father says, "You really cared about that turtle."

Below this second cartoon is another statement. "Parents don't usually give this kind of response, because they fear that by giving a name to the feeling, they'll make it worse. Just the opposite is true. The child who hears the words for what he is experiencing is deeply comforted. Someone has acknowledged his inner experience."[4]

In my own experience with my children and in my practice, I believe Faber and Mazlish are right on here. You will note in the example with the turtle that the authors did not use the format from Concept #1 and #3 because they take a slightly different approach, but it is essentially the same, using reflective listening or repeating back to the child what they heard the child say and feel.

Now that you have accurately identified feelings and emotions as well as the information the child is telling you, it is appropriate to give the child some honest encouragement and/or try to come up with a solution by asking the child to help by offering a solution. An example would be to say to the child the following regarding the situation above. "I bet if you practice you will get better and maybe you can try to get back in first Orchestra, if you want to. What do you think we should do about this?"

When we get to the point where we are sure we have good understanding we usually jump from here to concept #5 which is how to problem solve.

---

4   Faber, A. and Mazlish, E. (1999). *How To Talk So Kids Will Listen & Listen So Kids Will Talk*, P. 14-15. New York, NY: AVON BOOKS, INC.

CONCEPT #4

What to Do When You, the Parent, Is Upset?

This is what you do when you are upset about something the child has done: A skill to acquire.

- I feel (a feeling word or words)

- About (describe the behavior and be specific)

- Because (explain effects, your needs, motives, goals and values)

This should be pretty easy to do because you have already learned the same basic skill when the child is upset. Before you do this, however, you need to understand the next few concepts to make sure your statements to the child really work.

Be in Control of Your Emotions

Be Aware of Primary Feelings and Secondary Emotions

This is something you need to understand and use as a skill.

Before we go on you need to know that when you are upset and before you use any of the next steps you still need to be in control of your emotions. If you know you are not going to be emotionally in control, you need to give yourself some time to get in control. A time out away from the child is a good way to get a grip before you start this step. Be strong and promise yourself you won't proceed until you get your emotions in check, even if it takes an hour or two. In some extreme cases you might not be able to deal with a situation until you have had a good night's sleep. Of course, if there is a crisis situation where you need to deal with the child immediately then use the format below and later when things have calmed you can go back and discuss the matter in a controlled manner with a better frame of mind.

You will note that the format or paradigm as it is also called is basically the same in all examples in this chapter. When you are upset about what a child has done you need to let him or her know how that makes you feel by using the same format above, saying something like, "I feel ignored, unhappy, sad or disappointed, etc.," using a feeling word or words. This is *critical* because it is the best way to share what you are feeling without causing more damage to the relationship. Stating your feelings also softens the message and brings greater understanding to any situation. This works!

If we do what comes naturally we tend to use the road blocks above in concept #2, we become emotional and say things without thinking. When we use road blocks the other person/child often interprets this approach as an attack, causing the child or anyone to react negatively with anger or resentment. This usually causes them to feel justified and they continue with their negative attitude and behavior even if they know their behavior is inappropriate.

Right here I need to introduce a concept within a concept. It is twofold and called Primary Feelings and Secondary Emotions. Often when we are upset as parents we have a primary feeling which grows into a secondary emotion and that is when we get into trouble, by expressing our secondary emotion instead of the feeling we started with, the Primary Feeling. This is the key to staying in control. An example of this is when a teenager comes home an hour late from a date. As the scene begins, the parents are waiting for the child to return. When the child is 15 minutes late they start to become <u>concerned</u>. At 30 minutes late, they start to feel <u>worried</u>. At 45 minutes late, they are <u>fearful</u> and just before he/she comes home they are feeling <u>panic</u>. When the child walks in, he or she is greeted not with feelings of concern, worry, fear or panic (which are the primary feelings) instead, the child is confronted with the secondary emotions which are always in the range of resentment, anger, and even rage. Let's play this out in two different scenarios.

First Scenario with the Parent Expressing Secondary Emotions

The child walks in the door at 1:00 a.m. and says to the parents, "What are you doing up?" As if nothing is wrong. The parent says with an angry voice, expressing his secondary emotion of anger, "Do you know what time it is?" (Without waiting for a response.) "You're grounded for two weeks and will not drive the car." The teenager feels attacked and responds with secondary emotions of anger. "I don't care!" The child then throws the keys on the floor and storms off to his room.

Second Scenario with the Parent Expressing Primary Feelings

The child walks in the door at 1:00 a.m. and says, "What are you doing up?" As if nothing is wrong. The parent says with concern in his voice, but with total calmness and control. "We have been worried and afraid that something bad had happened to you because you are an hour late. We became so panicked when you did not answer your phone that we were about to call the police." Do you see how this approach is not an attack but it places the responsibility back on the child and provides the best climate for him or her to feel the weight of responsibility for their behavior? In this example the child is more likely to respond with an apology and regret than if one of the road-blocks to communication were used.

Now don't get testy here thinking that the child is getting off completely free without consequences. Once the parent and the child have the chance to say what they are thinking and feeling in a calm atmosphere then we get into choosing the consequences. Think of it this way. When people are brought before the court system to account for their behavior, the person is brought before the judge. He or she is not scolded by the judge; voices are not raised, and emotions are not in the blame or anger range. Defendants are told with respect and civility what they are accused of and then given the opportunity to respond to the charges and either take responsibility or attempt to explain the circumstances or their side of the story. If we could adopt the same method as the court system, in our families, when we need to deal with inappropriate behaviors from children, the outcomes would be overall much better. I CHALLENGE YOU to use this method of talking to your children whenever you have something unpleasant that needs to be addressed with your children. Just pretend you are in court and act as if the room is full of observers and a judge who will hear everything you say as the lead attorney. I am confident that if you do so you will experience a much better atmosphere and outcome. We will cover how to utilize appropriate consequences in Concept #7 so the child will learn appropriately from his or her mistakes.

CONCEPT #5

What to Do When There is Unity or When the Child Does Something Positive

This is a skill we need to develop. By doing the following you reinforce positive behavior, making it more likely that the child will repeat it again.

I feel (a feeling word or words like happy, sad, mad, glad or any other feeling)

About or when (describe the behavior and be specific)

Because (explain effects, your needs, motives, goals and values)

To describe what to do I will use two scenarios of a child's positive behavior. One is the child picks up her toys without being told. The second is a child who makes his bed without being reminded.

Note that you are using the same basic format as above.

Example #1- I feel happy about you picking up your toys without being reminded, because now we will have time to read a book before we go to the store.

Example #2- I feel relieved that you made your bed without being told, because I was not sure you would remember us talking about this last night. I am pleased because you showed me you are responsible. A little more added in there with two feeling words and comments.

Do you see how this flows and encourages the child to repeat his or her cooperative behavior? Granted, this is a process and does not always work immediately, but over time it will make a difference, if you are consistent and don't give up. As always, there are some exceptions to this. If you have a child who has special needs then you may need other help, but for most parents and children these and other basic parenting principles found in other parenting courses have proven themselves over many years to be successful with most children. Now you know what to do when you catch your child doing something right.

CONCEPT #6

No Lose Problem Solving

This is an important skill to develop as parents and practice with your children.

No Lose Problem Solving comes from a book called, *Parent Effectiveness Training in Action*, by Dr. Thomas Gordon.

I have used this process with parents, couples, and families with remarkable success for a long time. I will now explain how No Lose Problem Solving is applied with an example. I had a family who came to see me. The daughter was 16 and had not lived at home for about nine months. She was finally ready to meet with her parents and work on resolving their problems. One of the reasons she had left home is because she did not want her parents controlling her driving privileges. The first thing we did was to use communication as described above. When we completed the communication exercise, we identified three problems we needed to solve. The first problem was what kind of vehicle was going to be purchased. The second problem was who was going to pay for the vehicle. The third problem was what were the rules regarding her driving privileges.

Narrow down the problem to solve only one issue at a time. If there is more than one problem in an issue then each problem needs to be identified and problem solved individually.

Take a piece of paper and write the problem at the top. On the left side of the paper write down all the possible alternative solutions you can think of. On the right side place a column for each person involved.

Now you start brainstorming. This means thinking of any possible solution whether ridiculous or plausible. Every solution is written down no matter what it is. Here is how the actual example went regarding what kind of car this young woman would drive.

What Kind of Vehicle is She Going to Drive?

Solutions	Mom	Dad	Daughter
Mercedes			X
Corvette			X
(Several other nice cars were listed here)			X
$5000 car	X	X	X
$4000 car	X	X	X
$3000 car	X	X	
Full size truck	X	X	
(trucks from the family farm being sold)			
Small mini truck	X	X	X
(also from the family farm)			
Motorcycle			
Bicycle			
Tricycle			
Skateboard			
Roller skates			
Walk			

The next step is for each person to take the list and put a check by each solution they can live with. That is the important question each person must ask themselves. "What can I live with?" and only check those items. There is no arguing, no comments from anyone about what each person checks; they simply check or don't check. When everyone is finished, identify each option that was checked by all participants. Then you decide which solution you put into use. You will usually find there are three or more which are checked by all participants. Do you see how this process eliminates arguing and many other problems?

In this case, you will note the alternatives the mother, daughter and father all checked. They decided they would go with the small mini truck which was about to be sold from the farm. This made sense because there were no payments needed because it was owned by the family farm, and the daughter liked it because she thought it was small and cute. We went on to solve the two other problems regarding who would maintain the truck and the rules regarding the daughter's driving privileges.

The following is Dr. Gordon's detailed description of his method. I found this outline on the internet years ago and could not find the source for where this information is found. Any books or written material by Dr. Gordon is going to be worth your while and I encourage you to look for his books and order those you believe are related to your needs. As you get better at applying this great tool you would be wise to use these steps.

NO-LOSE PROBLEM SOLVING

From *P.E.T. In Action,* by Dr. Thomas Gordon

STEP 1: *Acknowledge & Express Feelings & Emotions* (Each person's feelings and emotions need to be acknowledged through "Reflective Listening" and each person needs to be able to express his or her feelings and emotions through the use of "I Messages".)

STEP 2: *Define the "Problem"* (What is reality and what is the problem? Who owns the problems?)

STEP 3: *Brainstorm Possible Solutions* (This means all parties involved generate Solutions; inventive, crazy, or wild ideas are included. All ideas are written down without comment.)

STEP 4: *Evaluate Possible Solutions*

STEP 5: *Decide on the Best Solution(s) or Plan of Action* (If appropriate write a contract outlining the agreed upon solutions, consequences and re-evaluation date. Have all parties read and sign it.)

STEP 6: *Implement the Plan*

STEP 7: *Re-Evaluate the Plan* (If the plan is working continue with it; if not modify as needed using the steps above.)

Conflicts of Needs Versus Conflicts of Values

It is important here to understand that this method of problem solving usually works well on conflicts of needs but not as well with conflicts of values. Let me define these terms. We all have needs and wants in our lives such as the need for food, shelter, and other goods that keep us alive, safe, and comfortable. We also have wants which are not generally necessary for sustaining life but they are our preferences, like wanting certain clothes, electronic gadgets, cars, etc. People also have beliefs, standards, or core values which are highly important to them and they are unlikely to change these beliefs. Examples of values are religious beliefs or the integrity a person has with regard to being honest or being unwilling to do something illegal or against a personal belief system.

You can see how it would be much easier to utilize No Lose Problem Solving when it comes to conflicts of needs as opposed to conflicts of values. This is because people are generally unwilling to change or compromise when it comes to their values. If there is a married couple, one of which believes it is okay to have extramarital relationships and the other believes in total fidelity, it will be very difficult if not impossible to resolve this situation with No Lose Problem Solving. Therefore, before you start using this method decide if you are dealing with conflicts of values or conflicts of needs. If you run into a conflict of values you might need to reevaluate your values, especially if those values are destructive to relationships. In such cases marriage counseling would be advisable. However, unless one or both spouses are willing to compromise, counseling will not be work.

A Few More Thoughts Regarding Using No Lose Problem Solving

If you get to a point where you have almost agreed on a solution for your conflict but you have not all checked the same solution you may want to do the following. I have seen cases in therapy sessions where we have used this method on subjects like curfews. For example, if we have on our list of options for curfew times 9:00, 10:00, 11:00 and 12:00 midnight. One parent has checked 10:00 and the other has checked 11:00. In this case we simply make a new list of curfew times from 10:00 to 10:15, 10:30, 10:45 and 11:00. Both parents checked the new options, and they both checked 10:30. You can also go to ten-minute increments as well and sometimes that is all it takes to find an option everyone can live with. Some people will stick to their guns and not budge for 15 or even 10 minutes. I ask these individuals, "Is it worth not coming up with a compromise for 15 or even 30 minutes, which will keep the conflict going on indefinitely?"

As Dr. Gordon indicates in step #7, reevaluate the plan, and I would recommend doing this once a week in most cases. If the solution it is not working then blame the plan not each other. Decide on a new plan, and if that does not work to your satisfaction then you may be at the point where it becomes apparent that one person is not putting effort into the plan. If it is a child then you go to the next concept (#7) and use Natural and Logical Consequences. If the unengaged person is an adult then he or she or everyone may need to seek counseling. It also may become very clear that someone does not really care to make changes and then other hard decisions might need to be made by the person or persons who are committed.

CONCEPT #7

Natural and Logical Consequences

This is another skill to develop as parents and practice on your children.

Natural and Logical Consequences are used when it becomes clear that the first four skills have not resulted in changing a child's inappropriate behavior.

The course I taught indicated that people learn best from life experiences. This is especially true when we experience what are called natural consequences. This is when we experience a consequence after doing something or sometimes after not doing anything at all, which produces a natural lesson for us. When we fail to put gas in our car it stops running. When we are angry and kick the wall we hurt our foot, producing pain and a hole to repair. When we don't go to bed until very late, we are tired the next day. When we don't go to work, we don't get paid or lose our job and so on. When the natural consequences are too harsh or dangerous for our children, we should think of a logical consequence to replace the dangerous one so no one gets hurt. An example of this would be if a child won't stay out of the street, then we take him or her inside or put the child in the backyard so the natural consequence (being hit by a car) does not happen. Thus, we have created a logical consequence so the child is safe. It is best if we can make the logical consequence as closely associated to the behavior as possible so the child makes a connection between his or her behavior and the consequence. The better we do this the less likely the child is to blame us for the consequence. For example, if children damage their toys they are told if they continue to damage them the toys will be removed and they will not be able to play with them. If this continues the parent needs to follow through and remove them. This teaches the child that you are true to your word. If a teenager comes in after curfew, he or she is not allowed to go out the next night or weekend, etc. A smart parent thinks about these consequences ahead of time, when the parent knows the child is likely to abuse his or her privileges. This way the parent is prepared and not caught off guard when a crisis happens. He or she is ready with a logical consequence and is calm and in control emotionally when the child comes in late. The parent even gives the child a warning of the possible consequences prior to the possible infraction. Be proactive.

CONSISTENCY

You will note I have put Consistency in capital letters. The reason that consistency is so important is that without it you are doomed to be played by children, even at surprisingly young ages. To understand more fully the importance of this principle, please read the paragraph, Consistency is Key to Parenting, in the chapter entitled, PARENTING AND CONCERNS WITH CHILDREN found in Book 1. Without this key principle you will make very little headway with your child or any relationship.

Put the Following Simplified Statements On a 3 x 5 Card to Help You Remember What to Do in Almost Any Situation

Wouldn't it be nice to have a brief outline you could carry in your pocket or have handy in your home to give you simple directions for almost any situation that comes up with your children? Well here it is.

The parenting course I taught could be whittled down to just a few statements on the front and back of a 3 x 5 card. There were five concepts that were the essence of the course. Four were placed on the front of the card and one on the back. The front of the card had an X from the top left corner down to the bottom right corner and from the bottom left corner to the top right corner. The four following statements are placed in each of the four spaces of the card as follows;

---

what to do when there is unity
(i.e. when the child does something you like and you want them to repeat)

I feel (*a feeling word*)

About or When

Because

what to do when you are upset	what to do when the child is upset
I feel (*a feeling word*)	I feel (*a feeling word*)
About or When	About or When
Because	Because

No Lose Problem Solving

On the back of the card is the statement;

If the Concepts and Skills on the Front of This Card Are Having No Effect in Changing the Child's Behavior Then Use This Next Concept

---

Natural and Logical Consequences

Now you have help for the majority of circumstances that face you day-by-day as a parent. Go ahead and make your card and then apply it with large doses of consistency on your part, and over time they will begin to work. I recommend that all parents take a parenting course to enhance their skills because we can all use more information when it comes to dealing with our children.

Where and How to Find Parenting Courses and Books on Parenting

Probably the most popular parenting class today is *Love and Logic*, also *123 Magic* but there are many more noteworthy resources. *Parenting from the Inside Out* and *The Whole-Brain Child,* are a little more intellectual and they also deal with your child's development. There are some good older parenting books out there like, *How to Talk so Children will Listen and Listen so Children will Talk*, *SOS* and *STEP* or *Systematic Techniques for Effective Parenting*. You can go to any book store and find many good titles including workbooks on the subject and, of course, online at one of the many websites who sell books. If you live in a rural area you might not have a parenting course available close by so the above books can be very helpful. Another option for those of you who live in small towns or isolated areas would be to take a course online. Do some searching and investigate various online courses to determine which more fully meets your needs. By far the most preferred method of learning other techniques of parenting is to attend a parenting course. I highly recommend this means of enhancing your parenting skills; it is just that much better in terms of how much you will get out of it.

To find a local course I recommend contacting your local schools or school district offices. By doing so you should be able to get some good information regarding courses being offered within the district or where to find a course. Another place to look would be your local mental health office who, often times, have these courses available.

Some hospitals run courses also. Ask your primary care doctor if they are aware of courses in your community. Your local health department may also know of where such courses are available. Searching the web is also good if you include the name of your town in the search.

Now you know what to do when a child is upset, when you are upset, and when the child does something you like and you want him or her to continue doing it. You also know how to solve problems and how to use natural and logical consequences more effectively. As I have indicated above, to make this easy just write these concepts down on a 3 by 5 card and carry it with you so whenever a situation arises and you don't quite know what to do, you can pull out the card and know how to better handle the situation. Go take a parenting course with a good attitude and it will be fun. If you do this, you will feel empowered and more confident in your ability to deal with your children. Good luck!

chapter thirteen

THIS AND THAT, WINDING UP

To finish this book, I have a few thoughts to share that don't particularly fit neatly into one chapter. They are given in no particular order, but I do feel they are helpful and important.

Finances

I mentioned this in the chapter on MARRIAGE COUNSELING WHAT IS IT LIKE, but I want to reemphasize it again. I believe we all need help with finances and I recommend taking the course called Financial Peace University. This is a nine-week program from Dave Ramsey's organization. This is an incredible course that teaches how to pay off debt, stay out of debt, establish an emergency fund, save/invest and then give back when you are in a position to do so. You can find a local class by going to his website at www.daveramsey.com. Mr. Ramsey has a bestselling book called, *The Total Money Makeover*, and everyone should have a copy of this book. He also has a radio show now heard across the U.S.

Trouble with the Law

If someone you love is in trouble with the law, do them a favor and make sure they have an attorney before talking to the police. This is always a very good idea. Trust me! If they can't afford an attorney, then they should wait to be assigned a public defender before speaking to law enforcement officers. Do all you can to make sure an attorney is there when someone is taken in for questioning. Some areas have poor public defender programs and access to one may be very limited. Many defense attorneys do some work for free, so calling defense attorneys might be worth the effort to inquire if they do such work. Don't confess to anything without an attorney present! If you can afford to hire an attorney, then by all means do so, because you will get the best representation. Where I live the basic rate for a criminal defense attorney is $5,000 up front, but it can make a huge difference in the life of someone who is accused of a crime. This is especially true if they can avoid a felony on their record. Don't trust anyone; just get an attorney.

Alcoholics Anonymous, Alanon:

Most people are aware that AA or Alcoholics Anonymous can be very helpful to those who struggle with drug and alcohol addiction. Less known is a program for loved ones or family members of addicts. This can be a very helpful and insightful program for anyone who is living with or is close to an addict. It is a 12-step program and is based on the same principles as AA. I would recommend this program to people who are dealing with someone with an addiction. This program can help people understand how to cope with an addict and provides support for people who are close to addicts. I believe it will make a real difference for anyone who attends. Look for these programs in your area with a web search or contact drug/alcohol treatment centers for this information. Addictions are huge problems now days and I have not addressed them because I don't treat them. I hope to do so in the future.

Feeling Word List

I am including a list of feeling words that can be used in parenting with children, marriage communication and counseling, or in any type of communication in life. As I have described in other chapters, using feeling words brings higher levels of understanding and insight into the minds of those who not only use them but especially to those who hear them and by doing so don't jump to conclusions. Feeling words also provide a softer sound to the ears of the receiver or the one who is listening. I promise if you use them your communication will be much better and more satisfying, as you say them and as you repeat them to the one you are listening to. Get good at this and you will feel validated and at the same time you will validate the other person.

excited	grateful	pleased	cherished
concern for	empty	discouraged	disappointed
worthless	powerless	inadequate	overwhelmed
incapable	uncertain	intimidated	desperate
panicked	threatened	alarmed	awkward
embarrassed	self-conscious	trapped	flustered
devastated	rejected	overlooked	criticized
mocked	unappreciated	furious	offended
vindictive	bugged	abandoned	lonely
left out	humiliated	exposed	ashamed
guilty	embarrassed	caring	hopeless

My advice is to use these feeling words in conjunction with the chapters, A BRIEF EXAMPLE OF A PARENTING COURSE, KEEPING THE MARRIAGE FRESH TAKES EFFORT, MARRIAGE COUNSELING HOW DOES IT WORK.

I sincerely hope this book has been helpful to all those who read it. There is so much more that could have been covered; however, I had to limit the material to make the length of the book manageable. Should this endeavor prove to be successful, I will consider addressing more topics in another version of this book.

Good luck and God bless you as you go forward in this beautiful and complicated world we live in.

NAVIGATING
LIFE
When and How to Involve a Professional

Book 1

In this book, you will discover what therapy is and how it helps heal anxiety, depression, PTSD, abuse and other mental, emotional problems. You will learn the difference between psychiatrists, psychologists and counselors and how medication works for mental health treatment. When you understand how counseling is done you will be more comfortable using the included suggestions for finding a counselor.

Book 2

In this book, you will learn about adoption, ADHD, autism, developmental delays in children and how to identify them, special needs, respite care and how to find special medical providers and primary care doctors. You will understand how to help your child using IEPs and 504 Accommodations and where to turn for support.

Book 3

In this book, you will learn about understanding personalities, fears, what to do prior to marriage, how to keep marriage working, the damage divorce causes, costs of going to counseling, why people don't go to counseling, what happens if they go or don't go, what marriage counseling is like, getting help in domestic abuse and the basics of parenting.

About the Author

With a degree in Psychology and Master's of Social Work, Craig has been practicing for 40 years in psychotherapy, marriage and family counseling. He has treated patients with varying mental/emotional disorders, including victims of sexual abuse. He was a foster parent for children with special needs and assisted parents who have children with special needs. He has worked with domestic and international adoptions for his entire career. He is the father of 7 children and 12 grandchildren. He loves being with his family and once this book is finished, he can't wait to get to the golf course.

Made in the USA
Monee, IL
11 April 2021